NOTICES

OF A

New Work

UPON

PARLIAMENTARY RULES,

BY

LUTHER S. CUSHING,

TWELVE YEARS CLERK OF THE MASSACHUSETTS HOUSE OF REPRESENTATIVES.

From Hon. S. H. Walley. Speaker of the Massachusetts House of Representatives.

ROXBURY, Jan. 13, 1845.

To the Publisher:

At your request, I have carefully perused the *Manual of Parliamentary Practice*, prepared by Hon. LUTHER S CUSHING, which you submitted in manuscript to my inspection.

I have taken great pleasure in examining the pages of this work, and do not hesitate to express most fully my approbation of its plan and execution.

On two or three questions of minor importance, I might come to different conclusions from the author;—but, inasmuch as he has devoted much time to a careful research into the subject of parliamentary rules and practice, in the preparation of an extended work, which he is preparing on this subject, I am free to admit, that I should feel great distrust in any opinions which I have held, even on these questions, where they differ from those expressed by Judge Cushing, without very careful reëxamination and study.

This Manual is much needed. There is no work, in this country, which is adapted near as well, in my judgment, to assist those who are called upon to preside in public assemblies, to discharge their duties acceptably and profitably to the community.

I sincerely hope and believe that this publication will receive the countenance and approbation to which it seems to me so justly entitled.

Very respectfully,
Your friend and servant,
SAMUEL H. WALLEY, Jr.

From the Law Reporter, Edited by Peleg W. Chandler, Esq., President of the Boston Common Council and Member of the Mass. Legislature.

Hon. LUTHER S. CUSHING has prepared for the press a new Manual of Parliamentary Practice. Having examined the manuscript of this work with considerable care, we take occasion to say, that it will be a valuable accession to the libraries of those who are called upon to preside in deliberative assemblies; and we believe the necessity of such a work as this has been very generally felt in our country, where almost every citizen is occasionally called upon to exercise the duties of a presiding officer. The work is founded upon the well-established rules and customs of the British Parliament, and Mr. Cushing divests himself of all local usages prevailing in different parts of this country; maintaining, in the outset, that no assembly can ever be subject to any other rules than those which are of general application, or which it specially adopts for its own government; and denying explicitly that the rules adopted and practised upon by a legislative assembly thereby acquire the character of general laws.

We understand that the author of this Manual has for some time been engaged on an elaborate treatise upon the parliamentary law, which we do not doubt will be creditable to his learning and industry. Meanwhile, this smaller and more convenient work will be sent out as a manual for practical reference.

Manual of Parliamentary Practice

RULES

OF

PROCEEDING AND DEBATE

IN

DELIBERATIVE ASSEMBLIES.

BY LUTHER S. CUSHING.

BOSTON:
WILLIAM J. REYNOLDS & CO.
1854.

ADVERTISEMENT TO THE SEVENTH EDITION.

Since the publication of the first edition of this work, in February, 1845, the author has endeavored, both by a careful revision of it himself, and by inquiries of others interested in the subject, to ascertain whether any alteration or addition was desirable, in order to render the work more useful for the purposes for which it was designed.

Certain alterations and additions have thus been suggested, which, though not numerous or very important, the author yet deems it his duty to make; and, for that purpose, to avail himself of the publication of the present edition.

The work being stereotyped, the new matter has not been incorporated with the original text, which would have rendered it necessary to recast the plates, but has been thrown into the form of notes, and placed at the end. It is hoped that these notes will add to the value and utility of the work; though it is not the intention of the publisher that they shall enhance its cost.

In the advertisement to the first edition of this work, the author announced that he was preparing a larger and more comprehensive work on parliamentary law and practice, which it was his intention to complete and publish as soon as possible. Inquiry having been frequently made, as to the time when the larger work would probably be published, the author takes this opportunity to say, that the little leisure which he has had at command, since the announcement alluded to, though diligently employed, has not as yet enabled him to finish that work. He is happy, however, to add, that nearly all the materials for it have been gathered together, and that the work itself is in a state of great forwardness, and will be completed and published, probably, in the course of the next year. To those who may find it difficult to conceive how so much time and labor can be required for the preparation of the work in question, it may not be improper to say, that, if completed on the plan which the author has adopted, it will form an octavo volume of not less, perhaps more, than five hundred pages.

Boston, November 1, 1847. L. S. C.

ADVERTISEMENT TO THE FIRST EDITION.

The following treatise forms a part only of a much larger and more comprehensive work, covering the whole ground of parliamentary law and practice, which the author has for some time been engaged in preparing; and which it his intention to complete and publish as soon as possible. In the meantime, this little work has been compiled, chiefly from the larger, at the request of the publishers, and to supply a want, which was supposed to exist to a considerable extent.

The treatise now presented to the public, is intended as a *Manual for Deliberative Assemblies* of every description, but more especially for those which are not legislative in their character; though, with the exception of the principal points, in which legislative bodies differ from others, namely, the several different stages or readings of a bill, and conferences and amendments between the two branches, this work will be found equally useful in legislative assemblies as in others.

The only work which has hitherto been in general use in this country, relating to the proceedings of legislative assemblies, is the compilation originally prepared by Mr. Jefferson, when Vice-President of the United States, for the use of the body over which he presided, and which is familiarly known as *Jefferson's Manual*. This work, having been extensively used in our legislative bodies, and, in some States, expressly sanctioned by law, may be said to form, as it were, the basis of the common parliamentary law of this country. Regarding it in that light, the author of the following treatise has considered the principles and rules laid down by Mr. Jefferson (and which have been adopted by him chiefly from the elaborate work of Mr. Hatsell) as the established rules on this subject, and has accordingly made them the basis of the present compilation, with an occasional remark, in a note, by way of explanation or suggestion, whenever he deemed it necessary.

Members of legislative bodies, who may have occasion to make use of this work, will do well to bear in mind, that it contains only what may be called the *common parliamentary law;* which, in every legislative assembly, is more or less modified or controlled by special rules.

Boston, November 1, 1844 L. S. C.

TABLE OF CONTENTS.

PARLIAMENTARY PRACTICE.

INTRODUCTION.

1. THE purposes, whatever they may be, for which a deliberative assembly of any kind is constituted, can only be effected by ascertaining the sense or will of the assembly, in reference to the several subjects submitted to it, and by embodying that sense or will in an intelligible, authentic, and authoritative form. To do this, it is necessary, in the first place, that the assembly should be properly constituted and organized; and, secondly, that it should conduct its proceedings according to certain rules, and agreeably to certain forms, which experience has shown to be the best adapted to the purpose.

2. Some deliberative assemblies, especially those which consist of permanently established

bodies, such as municipal and other corporations, are usually constituted and organized, at least, in part, in virtue of certain legal provisions; while others, of an occasional or temporary character, such as conventions and political meetings, constitute and organize themselves on their assembling together for the purposes of their appointment.

3. The most usual and convenient mode of organizing a deliberative assembly is the following. — The members being assembled together, in the place, and at the time, appointed for their meeting, one of them, addressing himself to the others, requests them to come to order; the members thereupon seating themselves, and giving their attention to him, he suggests the propriety and necessity of their being organized, before proceeding to business, and requests the members to nominate some person to act as chairman of the meeting; a name or names being thereupon mentioned, he declares that such a person (whose name was first heard by him) is nominated for chairman, and puts a question that the person so named be requested to take the chair. If this question should be decided in the negative, another nomination is then to

be called for, and a question put upon the name mentioned (being that of some other person) as before, and so on until a choice is effected. When a chairman is elected, he takes the chair, and proceeds in the same manner to complete the organization of the assembly, by the choice of a secretary and such other officers, if any, as may be deemed necessary.

4. An organization, thus effected, may be, and frequently is, sufficient for all the purposes of the meeting; but if, for any reason, it is desired to have a greater number of officers, or to have them selected with more deliberation, it is the practice to organize temporarily, in the manner above mentioned, and then to refer the subject of a permanent organization, and the selection of persons to be nominated for the several offices, to a committee; upon whose report, the meeting proceeds to organize itself, conformably thereto, or in such other manner as it thinks proper.

5. The presiding officer is usually denominated the *president*, and the recording officer, the *secretary*; though, sometimes, these officers are designated, respectively, as the *chairman* and *clerk*. It is not unusual, besides a president, to have one or more vice-presidents; who

take the chair, occasionally, in the absence of the president from the assembly, or when he withdraws from the chair to take part in the proceedings as a member; but who, at other times, though occupying seats with the president, act merely as members. It is frequently the case, also, that several persons are appointed secretaries, in which case, the first named is considered as the principal officer. All the officers are, ordinarily, members of the assembly[1]; and, as such, entitled to participate in the proceedings; except that the presiding officer does not usually engage in the debate, and votes only when the assembly is equally divided.

6. In all deliberative assemblies, the members of which are chosen or appointed to represent others, it is necessary, before proceeding to business, to ascertain who are duly elected and returned as members; in order not only that no person may be admitted to participate in the proceedings who is not regularly authorized to do so, but also that a

[1] In legislative bodies, the clerk is seldom or never a member; and, in some, the presiding officer is not a member; as, for example, in the Senate of the United States, the Senate of New York, and in some other state senates.

list of the members may be made for the use of the assembly and its officers.

7. The proper time for this investigation is after the temporary and before the permanent organization; or, when the assembly is permanently organized, in the first instance, before it proceeds to the transaction of any other business; and the most convenient mode of conducting it is by the appointment of a committee, to receive and report upon the credentials of the members. The same committee may also be charged with the investigation of rival claims, where any such are presented.

8. When a question arises, involving the right of a member to his seat, such member is entitled to be heard on the question, and he is then to withdraw from the assembly until it is decided; but if, by the indulgence of the assembly, he remains in his place, during the discussion, he ought neither to take any further part in it, nor to vote when the question is proposed; it being a fundamental rule of all deliberative assemblies, that those members, whose rights as such are not yet set aside, constitute a judicial tribunal to decide upon the cases of those whose rights of membership are called in question. Care should always

be taken, therefore, in the selection of the officers, and in the appointment of committees, to name only those persons whose rights as members are not objected to.

9. The place where an assembly is held being in its possession, and rightfully appropriated to its use, no person is entitled to be present therein, but by the consent of the assembly; and, consequently, if any person refuse to withdraw, when ordered to do so, or conduct himself in a disorderly or improper manner, the assembly may unquestionably employ sufficient force to remove such person from the meeting.

10. Every deliberative assembly, by the mere fact of its being assembled and constituted, does thereby necessarily adopt and become subject to those rules and forms of proceeding, without which it would be impossible for it to accomplish the purposes of its creation. It is perfectly competent, however, for every such body — and where the business is of considerable interest and importance, or likely to require some time for its accomplishment, it is not unusual — to adopt also certain special rules for the regulation of its proceedings. Where this is the case, these latter

supersede the ordinary parliamentary rules, in reference to all points to which they relate; or add to them in those particulars in reference to which there is no parliamentary rule; leaving what may be called the common parliamentary law in full force in all other respects.

11. The rules of parliamentary proceedings in this country are derived from, and essentially the same with, those of the British parliament; though, in order to adapt these rules to the circumstances and wants of our legislative assemblies, they have, in some few respects, been changed, — in others, differently applied, — and in others, again, extended beyond their original intention. To these rules, each legislative assembly is accustomed to add a code of its own, by which, in conjunction with the former, its proceedings are regulated. The rules, thus adopted by the several legislative assemblies, having been renewed in successive legislatures, — with such extensions, modifications and additions as have been, from time to time, thought necessary, — the result is, that a system of parliamentary rules has been established in each state, different in some particulars from those of every other state, but yet

founded in and embracing all the essential rules of the common parliamentary law.

12. The rules of proceeding, in each state, being of course best known by the citizens of that state, it has sometimes happened in deliberative assemblies, that the proceedings have been conducted not merely according to the general parliamentary law, but also in conformity with the peculiar system of the state in which the assembly was sitting, or of whose citizens it was composed. This, however, is erroneous; as no occasional assembly can ever be subject to any other rules, than those which are of general application, or which it specially adopts for its own government; and the rules adopted and practised upon by a legislative assembly do not thereby acquire the character of general laws.

13. The judgment, opinion, sense, or will of a deliberative assembly is expressed, according to the nature of the subject, either by a resolution, order, or vote. When it commands, it is by an *order;* but facts, principles, its own opinions, or purposes, are most properly expressed in the form of a *resolution;* the term *vote* may be applied to the result of every question decided by the assembly. In what-

ever form, however, a question is proposed, or by whatever name it may be called, the mode of proceeding is the same.

14. The judgment or will of any number of persons. considered as an aggregate body, is that which is evidenced by the consent or agreement of the greater number of them; and the only mode by which this can be ascertained, in reference to any particular subject, is, for some one of them to begin by submitting to the others a proposition, expressed in such a form of words, that, if assented to by the requisite number, it will purport to express the judgment or will of the assembly. This proposition will then form a basis for the further proceedings of the assembly; to be assented to, rejected, or modified, according as it expresses or not, or may be made to express, the sense of a majority of the members. The different proceedings which take place, from the first submission of a proposition, through all the changes it may undergo, until the final decision of the assembly upon it, constitute the subject of the rules of debate and proceeding in deliberative assemblies.

15. If the proceedings of a deliberative assembly were confined to the making of propo-

sitions by the individual members, and their acceptance or rejection by the votes of the assembly, there would be very little occasion for rules in such a body. But this is not the case. The functions of the members are not limited to giving an affirmative or negative to such questions as are proposed to them. When a proposition is made, if it be not agreed to or rejected at once, the assembly may be unwilling to consider and act upon it at all; or it may wish to postpone the consideration of the subject to a future time; or it may be willing to adopt the proposition with certain modifications; or, lastly, approving the subject-matter, but finding it presented in so crude, imperfect, or objectionable a form, that it cannot in that state be considered at all, the assembly may desire to have the proposition further examined and digested, before being presented. In order to enable the assembly to take whichever of the courses above indicated it may think proper, and then to dispose of every proposition in a suitable manner, certain motions or forms of question have been invented, which are perfectly adapted for the purpose, and are in common use in all deliberative assemblies.

CHAPTER I.

OF CERTAIN PRELIMINARY MATTERS.

16. Before entering upon the subject of the forms and rules of proceeding, in the transaction of business, it will be convenient to consider certain matters of a preliminary nature, which are more or less essential to the regularity, despatch, and efficiency of the proceedings.

SECTION I. QUORUM.

17. In all councils, [illegible] other collective bodies of the same kind, [illegible] necessary, that a certain number, called a quorum, of the members, should meet and be present, in order to the transaction of business. This regulation has been deemed essential to secure fairness of proceeding; and to prevent matters from being concluded in a hasty manner, or agreed to by so small a number of the members, as not to command a due and proper respect.

18. The number necessary to constitute a quorum of any assembly may be fixed by law,

as is the case with most of our legislative assemblies; or by usage, as in the English house of commons; or it may be fixed by the assembly itself; but if no rule is established on the subject, in any of these ways, a majority of the members composing the assembly is the requisite number.

19. No business can regularly be entered upon until a quorum is present; nor can any business be regularly proceeded with when it appears that the members present are reduced below that number; consequently, the presiding officer ought not to take the chair until the proper number is ascertained to be present; and if, at any time, in the course of the proceedings, notice is taken that a quorum is not present, and, upon the members being counted by the presiding officer, such appears to be the fact, the assembly must be immediately adjourned.

Sect. II. Rules and Orders.

20. Every deliberative assembly, as has already been observed, is, by the fact alone of its existence, subject to those rules of proceeding, without which it could not accomplish the purposes of its creation. It may also pro-

vide rules for itself, either in the form of a general code established beforehand, or by the adoption, from time to time, during its sitting, of such special rules as it may find necessary.

21. When a code of rules is adopted beforehand, it is usual also to provide therein as to the mode in which they may be amended, repealed, or dispensed with. Where there is no such provision, it will be competent for the assembly to act at any time, and in the usual manner, upon questions of amendment or repeal; but in reference to dispensing with a rule, or suspending it, in a particular case, if there is no express provision on the subject, it seems that it can only be done by general consent. [¶ 316.]

22. When any of the rules, adopted by the assembly, or in force, relative to its manner of proceeding, is disregarded or infringed, every member has the right to take notice thereof, and to require that the presiding officer, or any other whose duty it is, shall carry such rule into execution; and, in that case, the rule must be enforced, at once, without debate or delay. It is then too late to alter, repeal, or suspend the rule; so long as any one member insists upon its execution, it must be enforced.

Sect. III. Time of Meeting.

23. Every assembly, which is not likely to finish its business at one sitting, will find it convenient to come to some order or resolution beforehand, as to the time of reassembling, after an adjournment; it being generally embarrassing to fix upon the hour for this purpose, at the time when the sitting is about to close, and in connection with the motion to adjourn.

Sect. IV. Principle of Decision.

24. The principle, upon which the decisions of all aggregate bodies, such as councils, corporations, and deliberative assemblies, are made, is that of the majority of votes or suffrages; and this rule holds not only in reference to questions and subjects, which admit only of an affirmative on one side, and a negative on the other, but also in reference to elections in which more than two persons may receive the suffrages.

25. But this rule may be controlled by a special rule in reference to some particular subject or question; by which any less number

than a majority may be admitted, or any greater number required, to express the will of the assembly. Thus, it is frequently provided, in legislative assemblies, that one third or one fourth only of the members shall be sufficient to require the taking of a question by yeas and nays, and, on the other hand, that no alteration shall take place in any of the rules and orders, without the consent of at least two thirds, or even a larger number.

CHAPTER II.

OF THE OFFICERS.

26. The usual and necessary officers of a deliberative assembly are those already mentioned, namely, a presiding, and a recording, officer; both of whom are elected or appointed by the assembly itself, and removable at its pleasure. These officers are always to be elected by absolute majorities, even in those states in which elections are usually effected by a plurality; for the reason, that, being removable at the pleasure of the assembly, if any number short of a majority were to elect, a person elected by any such less number would not be able to retain his office for a moment; inasmuch as he might be instantly removed therefrom, on a question made for that purpose, by the votes of those who had voted for other persons on the election; and it is essential to the due and satisfactory performance of the functions of these officers, that they should possess the confidence of the assembly, which they cannot be said to do, unless they have the suffrages of at least a majority.

SECT. I. THE PRESIDING OFFICER.

27. The principal duties of this officer are the following: —

To open the sitting, at the time to which the assembly is adjourned, by taking the chair and calling the members to order;

To announce the business before the assembly in the order in which it is to be acted upon;

To receive and submit, in the proper manner, all motions and propositions presented by the members;

To put to vote all questions, which are regularly moved, or necessarily arise in the course of the proceedings, and to announce the result;

To restrain the members, when engaged in debate, within the rules of order;

To enforce on all occasions the observance of order and decorum among the members;

To receive all messages and other communications and announce them to the assembly;

To authenticate, by his signature, when necessary, all the acts, orders, and proceedings of the assembly;

To inform the assembly, when necessary, or when referred to for the purpose, in a point of order or practice;

To name the members (when directed to do so in a particular case, or when it is made a part of his general duty by a rule,) who are to serve on committees; and, in general,

To represent and stand for the assembly, declaring its will, and, in all things, obeying implicitly its commands.

28. If the assembly is organized by the choice of a president, and vice-presidents, it is the duty of one of the latter to take the chair, in case of the absence of the president from the assembly, or of his withdrawing from the chair for the purpose of participating in the proceedings.

29. Where but one presiding officer is appointed, in the first instance, his place can only be supplied, in case of his absence, by the appointment of a president or chairman *pro tempore;* and, in the choice of this officer, who ought to be elected before any other business is done, it is the duty of the secretary to conduct the proceedings.

30. The presiding officer may read sitting, but should rise to state a motion, or put a question to the assembly.

SECT. II. THE RECORDING OFFICER.

31. The principal duties of this officer consist in taking notes of all the proceedings, and in making true entries in his journal of all "the things done and past" in the assembly; but he is not, in general, required to take minutes of "particular men's speeches," or to make entries of things merely proposed or moved, without coming to a vote. He is to enter what is done and past, but not what is said or moved. This is the rule in legislative assemblies. In others, though the spirit of the rule ought to be observed, it is generally expected of the secretary, that his record shall be both a journal and in some sort a report of the proceedings.

32. It is also the duty of the secretary to read all papers, &c., which may be ordered to be read; to call the roll of the assembly, and take note of those who are absent, when a call is ordered; to call the roll and note the answers of the members, when a question is taken by yeas and nays; to notify committees of their appointment and of the business referred to them; and to authenticate by his signature (sometimes alone and sometimes in

conjunction with the president) all the acts, orders, and proceedings of the assembly.

33. The clerk is also charged with the custody of all the papers and documents of every description, belonging to the assembly, as well as the journal of its proceedings, and is to let none of them be taken from the table by any member or other person, without the leave or order of the assembly.

34. When but a single secretary or clerk is appointed, his place can only be supplied, during his absence, by the appointment of some one to act *pro tempore*. When several persons are appointed, this inconvenience is not likely to occur.

35. The clerk should stand while reading or calling the assembly.

CHAPTER III.

OF THE RIGHTS AND DUTIES OF THE MEMBERS.

36. The rights and duties of the members of a deliberative assembly, as regards one another, are founded in and derived from the principle of their absolute equality among themselves. Every member, however humble he may be, has the same right with every other, to submit his propositions to the assembly, — to explain and recommend them in discussion, — and to have them patiently examined and deliberately decided upon by the assembly; and, on the other hand, it is the duty of every one so to conduct himself, both in debate, and in his general deportment in the assembly, as not to obstruct any other member, in the enjoyment of his equal rights. The rights and duties of the members require to be explained only in reference to words spoken in debate (whether spoken of a member or otherwise) and to general deportment. The first will be most conveniently noticed in the chapter on debate the other will be considered in this place.

37. The observance of decorum, by the members of a deliberative assembly, is not only due to themselves and to one another, as gentlemen assembled together to deliberate on matters of common importance and interest, but is also essential to the regular and satisfactory proceeding of such an assembly. The rules on this subject, though generally laid down with reference to decorum in debate, are equally applicable whether the assembly be at the time engaged in debate, or not; and, therefore, it may be stated, generally, that no member is to disturb another, or the assembly itself, by hissing, coughing, or spitting; by speaking or whispering to other members; by standing up to the interruption of others; by passing between the presiding officer and a member speaking; going across the assembly room, or walking up and down in it; taking books or papers from the table, or writing there.

38. All these breaches of decorum are doubtless aggravated by being committed while the assembly is engaged in debate, though equally contrary to the rules of propriety, under any other circumstances. Assaults, by one member upon another, — threats, — challenges, — affrays, &c., are also high breaches of decorum.

39. It is also a breach of decorum for a member to come into the assembly room with his head covered, or to remove from one place to another with his hat on, or to put his hat on in coming in or removing, or, until he has taken his seat; and, in many assemblies, especially those which consist of a small number of members, it is not the custom to have the head covered at all.

40. In all instances of irregular and disorderly deportment, it is competent for every member, and is the special duty of the presiding officer, to complain to the assembly, or to take notice of the offence, and call the attention of the assembly to it. When a complaint of this kind is made by the presiding officer, he is said to *name* the member offending; that is, he declares to the assembly, that such a member, calling him by name, is guilty of certain irregular or improper conduct. The member, who is thus charged with an offence against the assembly, is entitled to be heard in his place in exculpation, and is then to withdraw. Being withdrawn, the presiding officer states the offence committed, and the assembly proceeds to consider of the degree and amount of punishment to be inflicted.

The assembly may allow the member com plained of to remain, when he offers to withdraw; or, on the other hand, it may require him to withdraw, if he do not offer to do so of his own accord. The proceedings are similar, when the complaint is made by a member, except that the offence is stated by such member, instead of being stated by the presiding officer.

41. No member ought to be present in the assembly, when any matter or business concerning himself is debating; nor, if present, by the indulgence of the assembly, ought he to vote on any such question. Whether the matter in question concern his private interest, or relate to his conduct as a member, — as for a breach of order, or for matter arising in debate, — as soon as it is fairly before the assembly, the member is to be heard in exculpation and then to withdraw, until the matter is settled. If, notwithstanding, a member should remain in the assembly and vote, his vote may and ought to be disallowed; it being contrary, not only to the laws of decency, but to the fundamental principle of the social compact, that a man should sit and act as a judge in his own case.

42. The only punishments, which can be inflicted upon its members by a deliberative assembly of the kind now under consideration, consist of reprimanding, — exclusion from the assembly, — a prohibition to speak or vote, for a specified time, — and expulsion; to which are to be added such other forms of punishment, as by apology, begging pardon, &c., as the assembly may see fit to impose, and to require the offender to submit to, on pain of expulsion.

CHAPTER IV.

OF THE INTRODUCTION OF BUSINESS.

43. The proceedings of a deliberative assembly, in reference to any particular subject, are ordinarily set in motion, in the first instance, by some one of the members either presenting a communication from persons not members, or himself submitting a proposition to the assembly.

44. Communications made to the assembly are of two kinds, namely, those which are merely for its information in matters of fact, and those which contain a request for some action on the part of the assembly, either of a general nature, or for the benefit of an individual. The latter only, as they alone constitute a foundation for future proceedings, require to be noticed.

45. Propositions made by members are drawn up and introduced, by motion, in the form which they are intended by the mover to bear, as orders, resolutions, or votes, if they should be adopted by the assembly. These

propositions, of whatever nature they may be, are usually denominated motions, until they are adopted; they then take the name which properly belongs to them.

46. When a member has occasion to make any communication whatever to the assembly, — whether to present a petition or other paper, or to make or second a motion of any kind, or merely to make a verbal statement, — as well as when one desires to address the assembly in debate, he must, in the first place, as the expression is, "obtain the floor" for the purpose he has in view. In order to do this, he must rise in his place[1], and, standing uncovered, address himself to the presiding officer, by his title; the latter, on hearing himself thus addressed, calls to the member by his name; and the member may then, but not before, proceed with his business.

47. If two or more members rise and address themselves to the presiding officer, at the same time, or nearly so, he should give

---

[1] In the house of representatives of Massachusetts, where each member's seat is regularly assigned to him, and numbered, it has been found useful, in deciding upon the claims of several competitors for the floor, to prefer one who rises in his place, to a member who addresses the speaker from the area, the passageways, or the seat of any other member.

the floor to the member, whose voice he first heard. If his decision should not be satisfactory, any member may call it in question, saying that in his opinion such a member (not the one named) was first up, and have the sense of the assembly taken thereon, as to which of the members should be heard. In this case, the question should be first taken upon the name of the member announced by the presiding officer; and, if this question should be decided in the negative, then upon the name of the member for whom the floor was claimed in opposition to him.

48. The mode of proceeding upon such communications from persons not members, as are above alluded to, may be explained by that adopted on the presentation of a petition, which may be considered as the representative of the whole class to which it belongs.

49. A petition, in order to be received, should be subscribed by the petitioner himself, with his own hand, either by name or mark, except in case of inability from sickness, or because the petitioner is attending in person; and should be presented or offered, not by the petitioner himself, but by some member to whom it is intrusted for that purpose.

50. The member, who presents a petition, should previously have informed himself of its contents, so as to be able to state the substance of it, on offering it to the assembly, and also to be prepared to say, if any question should be made, that in his judgment it is couched in proper language, and contains nothing intentionally disrespectful to the assembly.

51. Being thus prepared, the member rises in his place, with the petition in his hand, and informs the assembly that he has a certain petition, stating the substance of it, which he thereupon presents or offers to the assembly, and, at the same time moves (which, however, may be done by any other member) that it be received; this motion being seconded, the question is put whether the assembly will receive the petition or not. This is the regular course of proceeding; but, in practice, there is seldom any question made on receiving a petition; the presiding officer usually taking it for granted, that there is no objection to the reception, unless it be stated. If, however, any objection is made to a petition, before it has been otherwise disposed of, the presiding officer ought to retrace his steps and require a motion of reception to be regularly made and seconded. [¶ 317.]

52. If the question of reception is determined in the affirmative, the petition is brought up to the table by the member presenting it; and is there read as of course by the clerk. It is then regularly before the assembly, to be dealt with as it thinks proper; the usual course being either to proceed to consider the subject of it immediately, or to assign some future time for its consideration, or to order it to lie on the table for the examination and consideration of the members individually.

53. Whenever a member introduces a proposition of his own, for the consideration of the assembly, he puts it into the form he desires it should have, and then moves that it be adopted as the resolution, order, or vote of the assembly. If this proposition so far meets the approbation of other members, that one of them rises in his place and seconds it, it may then be put to the question; and the result, whether affirmative or negative, becomes the judgment of the assembly.

54. A motion must be submitted in writing; otherwise the presiding officer will be justified in refusing to receive it; he may do so, however, if he pleases, and is willing to take the trouble himself to reduce it to writing. This

rule extends only to principal motions, which, when adopted, become the act and express the sense of the assembly; but not to subsidiary or incidental motions[1] which merely enable the assembly to dispose of the former in the manner it desires, and which are always in the same form. In the case of a motion to amend, which is a subsidiary motion, the rule admits of an exception, so far as regards the insertion of additional words, which, as well as the principal motion, must be in writing.

55. A motion must also be seconded, that is, approved by some one member, at least, expressing his approval by rising and saying, that he seconds the motion; and if a motion be not seconded, no notice whatever is to be taken of it by the presiding officer; though, in practice, very many motions, particularly those which occur in the ordinary routine of business, are admitted without being seconded. This rule applies as well to subsidiary as principal motions. The seconding of a motion seems to be required, on the ground, that the time of the assembly ought not to be taken up by a question, which, for any thing that appears,

[1] Such as, to adjourn, — lie on the table, — for the previous question, — for postponement, — commitment, &c.

has no one in its favor but the mover. There are some apparent exceptions to this rule, which will be stated hereafter, in those cases, in which one member alone has the right of instituting or giving direction to a particular proceeding; and an actual exception is sometimes made by a special rule, requiring certain motions to be seconded by more than one member. [¶ 318.]

56. When a motion has been made and seconded, it is then to be stated by the presiding officer to the assembly, and thus becomes a question for its decision; and, until so stated, it is not in order for any other motion to be made, or for any member to speak to it; but, when moved, seconded, and stated from the chair, a motion is in the possession of the assembly, and cannot be withdrawn by the mover, but by special leave of the assembly, which must be obtained by a motion made and seconded as in other cases. [¶ 319.]

57. When a motion is regularly before the assembly, it is the duty of the presiding officer to state it, if it be not in writing, or to cause it to be read, if it be, as often as any member desires to have it stated or read for his information.

58. When a motion or proposition is regularly before the assembly, no other motion can be received, unless it be one which is previous in its nature to the question under consideration, and consequently entitled to take its place for the time being, and be first decided.

CHAPTER V.

OF MOTIONS IN GENERAL.

59. When a proposition is made to a deliberative assembly, for its adoption, the proposition may be in such a form as to be put to the question, and the assembly may be in such a state as to be willing to come to a decision upon it, at once; and when this is the case, nothing more can be necessary than to take the votes of the members, and ascertain the result. But a different state of things may and commonly does exist; the assembly may prefer some other course of proceeding to an immediate decision of the question in the form in which it is presented; and, as it is proper, that every parliamentary body should have the means of fitly disposing of every proposition which may be made to it, certain forms of question have from time to time been invented, and are now in general use, for that purpose. These forms of question may properly be called *subsidiary*, in order to distinguish them from the principal motion or question to which they relate.

60. The different states of mind, in which a proposition may be received by a deliberative assembly, and the corresponding forms of proceeding, or subsidiary motions, to which they give rise, in order to ascertain the sense of the assembly, are the following: —

First. The assembly may look upon the proposition as useless or inexpedient; and may therefore desire to suppress it, either for a time, or altogether. The subsidiary motions, for this purpose, are the previous question and indefinite postponement.

Second. The assembly may be willing to entertain and consider of a proposition, but not at the time when it is made; either because more information is wanted by the members individually; or because they desire further time for reflection and examination; or because the assembly is then occupied with some other matter, which has more pressing claims upon its present attention. The usual motions, under such circumstances, are postponement to some future day or time, and to lie on the table.

Third. The subject-matter of a proposition may be regarded with favor, but the form in which it is introduced may be so defective, that a more careful and deliberate consideration, than can conveniently be given to it in the assembly itself, may be necessary to put it into a satisfactory form. In this case, it is most proper to refer the proposition to a committee.

Fourth The proposition may be acceptable, and the form in which it is presented so far satisfactory, that the assembly may be willing to consider and act upon it, with such alterations and amendments as may be thought proper. The motion adapted to this case is to amend.

61. It is not to be supposed, that the subsidiary motions above specified are the only ones that have at any time been adopted or used; or that it is not competent to a deliberative assembly to frame new motions at pleasure; but these are the forms in most common use, and are entirely sufficient for all practical purposes[1]. Neither is it to be sup-

[1] It is usual, in legislative assemblies, to provide by a special rule, both as to the particular motions to be used, and the order in which they may be made. Thus, the rule in the house of representatives of congress, (which is also adopted in the house of representatives of Massachusetts,) is, that, "when a question is under debate, no motion shall be received, but to adjourn, to lie on the table, for the previous question, to postpone to a day certain, to commit, to amend, to postpone indefinitely, which several motions shall have precedence in the order in which they are arranged."

posed, that these motions are always applied strictly to the cases to which they most appropriately belong; several of them are frequently used to effect purposes, for which others would be more proper. These misapplications will be taken notice of, under the heads of the several motions.

CHAPTER IV.

OF MOTIONS TO SUPPRESS.

62. When a proposition is moved, which, it is supposed, may be regarded by the assembly as useless or inexpedient, and which it may therefore be desirous to get rid of, such proposition may be suppressed for a time by means of the previous question, or altogether by a motion for indefinite postponement.

Sect. I. Previous Question.

63. The original and proper parliamentary use of the previous question being, as above stated, the suppression of a main question, it seems proper to consider it as one of the subsidiary motions for that purpose; although, in this country, it has been perverted to a wholly different use, namely, the suppression of debate. This consideration, in connection with the difficulty of the subject, and the importance of a correct understanding of it, makes it proper to devote more room to the previous question, than needs to be given to most of the other

subsidiary motions. It will first be considered according to its original use and intention; and, afterwards, as used in this country.

64. There are several motions, which give rise to questions previous in their nature to other questions to which they relate; but the term *previous* has been applied exclusively to a motion denominated the *previous question*, which has for its object the suppression of a principal motion or question. This motion was introduced into the house of commons, in England, more than two centuries ago, for the purpose of suppressing subjects of a delicate nature, relating to high personages, or the discussion of which might call forth observations of an injurious tendency. When first made use of, the form of the motion was, *shall the main question be put?* and the effect of a decision of it in the negative was to suppress the main question for the whole session. The form of it was afterwards changed to that which it has at present, namely, *shall the main question be now put?* and the effect of a negative decision of it now is to suppress the main question for the residue of the day only. The operation of this motion, in suppressing the

question to which it is applied, results from the principle, that no further consideration or discussion can regularly be had of a subject, which it has been decided shall not be put to the question; and, therefore, when, on the motion of the previous question, it has been decided, that the principal question shall not now be put, that question is disposed of for the day, and cannot be renewed until the next or some succeeding day. This is the purpose for which the previous question was originally invented, and for which it is still used in the British parliament.

65. But the previous question may be decided in the affirmative, as well as the negative, that is, that the main question shall now be put; in which case, that question is to be put immediately, without any further debate, and in the form in which it then exists. This operation of the previous question, when decided affirmatively, has led to the use of it for the purpose of suppressing debate on a principal question, and coming to a vote upon it immediately; and this is ordinarily the only object of the previous question, as made use of in the legislative assemblies of the United

States[1]. The operation of a negative decision is different in different assemblies; in some, as, for example, in the house of representatives of congress, it operates to dispose of the principal or main question by suppressing or removing it from before the house for the day; but in others, as in the house of representatives of Massachusetts, and in the house of assembly of New York, (in the former by usage only, and in the latter by a rule,) the effect of a negative decision of the previous question is to leave the main question under debate for the residue of the sitting, unless sooner disposed of, by taking the question, or in some other manner.

66. In England, the previous question is used only for suppressing a main question; the object of the mover is to obtain a decision of it in the negative; and the effect of such a decision, though in strictness only to suppress the question for the day, is, practically and by

---

[1] Mr. Jefferson (*Manual*, § xxxiv.) considers this extension of the previous question as an abuse. He is of opinion, that "its uses would be as well answered by other more simple parliamentary forms, and therefore it should not be favored, but restricted within as narrow limits as possible." Notwithstanding this suggestion, however, the use of the previous question, as above stated, has become so firmly established, that it cannot now be disturbed or unsettled.

parliamentary usage, to dispose of the subject altogether. In this country, the previous question is used chiefly for suppressing debate on a main question; the object of the mover is to obtain a decision of it in the affirmative; and the effect of a decision the other way, though in some assemblies operating technically to suppress the main question for the day only, is, in general, merely to suspend the taking of the question for that day; either leaving the debate to go on during the residue of the day, or the subject to be renewed on the next or some other day. The operation of an affirmative decision is the same, in both countries, namely, the putting of the main question immediately, and without further debate, delay, or consideration.

SECT. II. INDEFINITE POSTPONEMENT.

67. In order to suppress a question altogether, without coming to a direct vote upon it, in such a manner that it cannot be renewed the proper motion is for indefinite postponement; that is, a postponement or adjournment of the question, without fixing any day for resuming it. The effect of this motion, if decided

in the affirmative, is to quash the proposition entirely; as an indefinite adjournment is equivalent to a dissolution, or the continuance of a suit, without day, is a discontinuance of it. A negative decision has no effect whatever.

CHAPTER VII.

OF MOTIONS TO POSTPONE.

68. If the assembly is willing to entertain and consider a question, but not at the time when it is moved, the proper course is either to postpone the subject to another day, or to order it to lie on the table.

69. When the members individually want more information than they possess, at the time a question is moved, or desire further time for reflection and examination, the proper motion is, to postpone the subject to such future day as will answer the views of the assembly.

70. This motion is sometimes used improperly, to get rid of a proposition altogether, as would be done by an indefinite postponement. This is effected by fixing upon a day, which, according to the common course of things, will not arrive until after the assembly has been brought to a close. But a motion, worded in this manner, is precisely equivalent to a motion for indefinite postponement, and should be so considered and treated.

71. If the assembly has something else before it, which claims its present attention, and is therefore desirous to postpone a particular proposition, until that subject is disposed of, such postponement may be effected by means of a motion that the matter in question lie on the table. If this motion prevails, the subject so disposed of may be taken up, at any time afterwards, and considered, when it may suit the convenience of the assembly. [¶ 320.]

72. This motion is also sometimes made use of for the final disposition of a subject; and, it always has that effect, when no motion is afterwards made to take it up.

CHAPTER VIII.

OF MOTIONS TO COMMIT.

73. The third case for the use of a subsidiary motion, as already stated, occurs, when the subject-matter of a proposition is regarded with favor, but the form in which it is introduced is so defective, that a more careful and deliberate consideration is necessary, than can conveniently be given to it in the assembly itself, in order to put it into a satisfactory form. The course of proceeding then is, to refer the subject to a committee; which is called a commitment, or, if the subject has already been in the hands of a committee, a recommitment.

74. If there is a standing committee of the assembly, whose functions embrace the subject in question, the motion should be to refer it tc that committee; if there is no such committee, then the motion should be to refer to a select committee. If it is a matter of doubt, whether a particular standing committee is appropriate or not, and propositions are made for a reference to that committee, and also for a reference to

a select committee, the former proposition should be first put to the question.

75. When a subject is referred or recommitted, the committee may be instructed or ordered by the assembly, as to any part or the whole of the duties assigned them; or the subject may be left with them without instructions. In the former case, the instructions must be obeyed, of course; in the latter, the committee have full power over the matter, and may report upon it, in any manner they please, provided they keep within the recognized forms of parliamentary proceedings. [¶ 321.]

76. A part only of a subject may be committed, without the residue; or different parts may be committed to different committees.

77. A commitment with instructions is sometimes made use of, as a convenient mode of procuring further information, and, at the same time, of postponing the consideration of a subject to a future though uncertain day.

CHAPTER IX.

OF MOTIONS TO AMEND.

78. The last case, for the introduction of subsidiary motions, is when the assembly is satisfied with the subject-matter of a proposition, but not with the form of it, or with all its different parts, or desires to make some addition to it. The course of proceeding then is, to bring the proposition into the proper form, and make its details satisfactory, by means of amendments, or of certain proceedings of a similar character, and having the same general purpose in view. The latter will be first considered.

SECT. I. DIVISION OF A QUESTION.

79. When a proposition or motion is complicated, that is, composed of two or more parts, which are so far independent of each other, as to be susceptible of division into several questions, and it is supposed that the assembly may approve of some but not of all these parts, it is a compendious mode of

amendment, to divide the motion into separate questions, to be separately voted upon and decided by the assembly. This division may take place by the order of the assembly, on a motion regularly made and seconded for the purpose.

80. When a motion is thus divided, it becomes a series of questions, to be considered and treated each by itself, as an independent proposition, in the order in which they stand; and when they have all been gone through with and decided, the result will be the same, as if motions to amend by striking out the several parts had been made and put to the question. When a motion for a division is made, the mover ought to specify in his motion the manner in which he proposes to make the division; and this motion, like every other of the nature of an amendment, is itself susceptible of amendment.

81. It is sometimes asserted, that it is the right of every individual member to have a complicated question (provided it is susceptible of division) divided into its several parts, and a question put separately on each, on his mere demand, and without any motion or any vote of the assembly for that purpose. But this is a

mistake; there is no such rule of parliamentary proceeding; a complicated question can only be separated by moving amendments to it in the usual manner, or by moving for a division of it in the manner above stated.

82. It is not unusual, however, for a deliberative assembly to have a rule providing for the division of a complicated question (provided it is susceptible of division) into its several parts, upon the demand of a member. When this is the case, it is for the presiding officer (subject of course to the revision of the assembly) to decide, when the division of a motion is demanded, first, whether the proposition is susceptible of division, and, secondly, into how many and what parts it may be divided.

83. A proposition, in order to be divisible, must comprehend points so distinct and entire, that if one or more of them be taken away, the others may stand entire and by themselves; but a qualifying paragraph, as, for example, an exception or a proviso, if separated from the general assertion or statement to which it belongs, does not contain an entire point or proposition.

Sect. II. Filling Blanks.

84. It often happens, that a proposition is introduced with blanks purposely left by the mover to be filled by the assembly, either with times and numbers, or with provisions analogous to those of the proposition itself. In the latter case, blanks are filled in the same way, that other amendments by the insertion of words are made. In the former, propositions to fill blanks are not considered as amendments to the question, but as original motions, to be made and decided before the principal question.

85. When a blank is left to be filled with a time or number, motions may be made for that purpose, and the question taken on each by itself, and before another is made; or several motions may be made and pending before any of them are put to the question. This last mode of proceeding, which is the most usual as well as convenient, requires that the several propositions should be arranged, and the question taken on them, in such order as will the soonest and with the most certainty enable the assembly to come to an agreement.

86. In determining upon the order to be adopted, the object is not to begin at that ex-

treme, which and more being within every man's wish, no one can vote against it, and, yet, if it should be carried in the affirmative, every question for more would be precluded: but, at that extreme, which will be likely to unite the fewest, and then to advance or recede, until a number or time is reached, which will unite a majority.

87. Hence, when several different propositions are made for filling blanks with a time or number, the rule is, that if the *larger* comprehends the *lesser*, as in a question to what day a postponement shall take place, — the number of which a committee shall consist, — the amount of a fine to be imposed, — the term of an imprisonment, — the term of irredeemability of a loan, — or the *terminus in quem* in any other case, the question must begin *a maximo*, and be first taken upon the greatest or farthest, and so on to the least or nearest, until the assembly comes to a vote: But, if the *lesser* includes the *greater*, as in questions on the limitation of the rate of interest, — on the amount of a tax, — on what day the session of a legislative assembly shall be closed, by adjournment, — on what day the next session shall commence, — or the *terminus a quo* in

any other case, the question must begin *a minimo*, and be first taken on the least or nearest, and so on to the greatest or most remote, until the assembly comes to a vote[1].

SECT. III. ADDITION, — SEPARATION, — TRANSPOSITION.

88. When the matters contained in two separate propositions might be better put into one, the mode of proceeding is, to reject one of them, and then to incorporate the substance of it with the other by way of amendment. A better mode, however, if the business of the assembly will admit of its being adopted, is to refer both propositions to a committee, with instructions to incorporate them together in one.

89. So, on the other hand, if the matter of one proposition would be more properly distributed into two, any part of it may be struck out by way of amendment, and put into the

---

[1] The above is the rule as laid down by Mr. Jefferson (§ 33), and holds where it is not superseded by a special rule, which is generally the case in our legislative assemblies; as, for example, in the senate of the United States, the rule is, that in filling blanks, the *largest* sum and *longest* time shall be first put. In the house of commons, in England, the rule established by usage is, that the *smallest* sum and the *longest* time shall be first put.

form of a new and distinct proposition. But, in this, as in the former case, a better mode would generally be to refer the subject to a committee.

90. In like manner, if a paragraph or section requires to be transposed, a question must be put on striking it out where it stands, and another for inserting it in the place desired.

91. The numbers prefixed to the several sections, paragraphs, or resolutions, which constitute a proposition, are merely marginal indications, and no part of the text of the proposition itself; and, if necessary, they may be altered or regulated by the clerk, without any vote or order of the assembly.

SECT. IV. MODIFICATION OR AMENDMENT BY THE MOVER.

92. The mover of a proposition is sometimes allowed to modify it, after it has been stated as a question by the presiding officer; but, as this is equivalent to a withdrawal of the motion, in order to substitute another in its place; and, since, as has already been seen, a motion regularly made, seconded, and proposed, cannot be withdrawn without leave; it is clear,

that the practice alluded to rests only upon general consent; and, that, if objected to, the mover of a proposition must obtain the permission of the assembly, by a motion and question for the purpose, in order to enable him to modify his proposition.

93. So, too, when an amendment has been regularly moved and seconded, it is sometimes the practice for the mover of the proposition to which it relates to signify his consent to it, and for the amendment to be thereupon made, without any question being taken upon it by the assembly. As this proceeding, however, is essentially the same with that described in the preceding paragraph, it, of course, rests upon the same foundation, and is subject to the same rule. [¶ 322.]

Sect. V. General Rules relating to Amendments.

94. All amendments, of which a proposition is susceptible, so far as form is concerned, may be effected in one of three ways, namely, either by inserting or adding certain words; or by striking out certain words; or by striking out certain words, and inserting or adding

others. These several forms of amendment are subject to certain general rules, which, being equally applicable to them all, require to be stated beforehand.

95. *First Rule.* When a proposition consists of several sections, paragraphs, or resolutions, the natural order of considering and amending it is to begin at the beginning, and to proceed through it in course by paragraphs; and when a latter part has been amended, it is not in order to recur back, and make any alteration or amendment of a former part.

96. *Second Rule.* Every amendment, which can be proposed, whether by striking out, or inserting, or striking out and inserting, is itself susceptible of amendment; but there can be no amendment of an amendment to an amendment; this would be such a piling of questions one upon another, as would lead to great embarrassment; and as the line must be drawn somewhere, it has been fixed by usage after the amendment to the amendment. The object, which is proposed to be effected by such a proceeding, must be sought by rejecting the amendment to the amendment, in the form in which it is proposed, and then moving it again in the form in which it is wished to be

amended, in which it is only an amendment to an amendment; and in order to accomplish this, he who desires to amend an amendment should give notice, that, if rejected, in the form in which it is presented, he shall move it again in the form in which he desires to have it adopted.

97. Thus, if a proposition consist of A B, and it is proposed to amend by inserting C D, it may be moved to amend the amendment by inserting E F; but it cannot be moved to amend this amendment, as, for example, by inserting G. The only mode, by which this can be reached, is to reject the amendment in the form in which it is presented, namely, to insert E F, and to move it in the form in which it is desired to be amended, namely, to insert E G F.

98. *Third Rule.* Whatever is agreed to by the assembly, on a vote, either adopting or rejecting a proposed amendment, cannot be afterwards altered or amended.

99. Thus, if a proposition consist of A B, and it is moved to insert C; if the amendment prevail, C cannot be afterwards amended, because it has been agreed to in that form; and, so, if it is moved to strike out B, and the

5

amendment is rejected, B cannot afterwards be amended, because a vote against striking it out is equivalent to a vote agreeing to it as it stands.

100. *Fourth Rule.* Whatever is disagreed to by the assembly, on a vote, cannot be afterwards moved again. This rule is the converse of the preceding, and may be illustrated in the same manner.

101. Thus, if it is moved to amend A B by inserting C, and the amendment is rejected, C cannot be moved again; or, if it is moved to amend A B by striking out B, and the amendment prevails, B cannot be restored, because, in the first case, C, and, in the other, B, have been disagreed to by a vote.

102. *Fifth Rule* The inconsistency or incompatibility of a proposed amendment with one which has already been adopted, is a fit ground for its rejection by the assembly, but not for the suppression of it by the presiding officer, as against order; for, if questions of this nature were allowed to be brought within the jurisdiction of the presiding officer, as matters of order, he might usurp a negative on important modifications, and suppress or embarrass instead of subserving the will of the assembly.

SECT. VI. AMENDMENTS BY STRIKING OUT.

103. If an amendment is proposed by striking out a particular paragraph or certain words, and the amendment is rejected, it cannot be again moved to strike out the same words or a part of them; but it may be moved to strike out the same words with others, or to strike out a part of the same words with others, provided the coherence to be struck out be so substantial, as to make these, in fact, different propositions from the former.*

104. Thus, if a proposition consist of A B C D, and it is moved to strike out B C; if this amendment is rejected, it cannot be moved again; but it may be moved to strike out A B, or A B C, or B C D or C D.

105. If an amendment by striking out is agreed to, it cannot be afterwards moved to insert the same words struck out or a part of them; but it may be moved to insert the same words with others, or a part of the same words with others, provided the coherence to be inserted make these propositions substantially different from the first.

106. Thus, if the proposition A B C D is amended by striking out B C, it cannot be

moved to insert B C again; but it may be moved to insert B C with other words, or B with others, or C with others.

107. When it is proposed to amend by striking out a particular paragraph, it may be moved to amend this amendment, in three different ways, namely, either by striking out a part only of the paragraph, or by inserting or adding words, or by striking out and inserting.

108. Thus, if it is moved to amend the proposition A B C D, by striking out B C, it may be moved to amend this amendment by striking out B only or C only, or by inserting E, or by striking out B or C, and inserting E.

109. In the case of a proposed amendment by striking out, the effect of voting upon it, whether it be decided in the affirmative or negative, according to the third and fourth rules above mentioned, renders it necessary for those who desire to retain the paragraph to amend it, if any amendment is necessary, before the vote is taken on striking out; as, if struck out, it cannot be restored, and, if retained, it cannot be amended.

110. As an amendment must necessarily be put to the question before the principal motion;

so the question must be put on an amendment to an amendment before it is put on the amendment; but, as this is the extreme limit to which motions may be put upon one another, there can be no precedence of one over another among amendments to amendments; and, consequently, they can only be moved, one at a time, or, at all events, must be put to the question in the order in which they are moved.

111. When a motion for striking out words is put to the question, the parliamentary form always is, whether the words *shall stand as part* of the principal motion, and not whether they *shall be struck out*. The reason for this form of stating the question probably is, that the question may be taken in the same manner on a part as on the whole of the principal motion; which would not be the case, if the question was stated on striking out; inasmuch as the question on the principal motion, when it comes to be stated, will be on agreeing to it, and not on striking out or rejecting it. Besides, as an equal division of the assembly would produce a different decision of the question, according to the manner of stating it, it might happen, if the question on the amend

ment was stated on striking out, that the same question would be decided both affirmatively and negatively by the same vote[1].

112. On a motion to amend by striking out certain words, the manner of stating the question is, first to read the passage proposed to be amended, as it stands; then the words proposed to be struck out; and, lastly, the whole passage as it will stand if the amendment is adopted. [¶ 323.]

SECT. VII. AMENDMENTS BY INSERTING.

113. If an amendment is proposed by inserting or adding a paragraph or words, and the amendment is rejected, it cannot be moved again to insert the same words or a part of them; but it may be moved to insert the same words with others, or a part of the same words with others, provided the coherence really make them different propositions.

114. Thus, if it is moved to amend the proposition A B by inserting C D, and the amendment is rejected, C D cannot be again moved;

---

[1] The common, if not the only, mode of stating the question, in the legislative assemblies of this country, is on *striking out.*

but it may be moved to insert C E, or D E, or C D E.

115. If it is proposed to amend by inserting a paragraph, and the amendment prevails, it cannot be afterwards moved to strike out the same words or a part of them; but it may be moved to strike out the same words with others[1], or a part of the same words with others, provided the coherence be such as to make these propositions really different from the first.

116. Thus, if in the example above supposed, the amendment prevails, and C D is inserted, it cannot be afterwards moved to strike out C D, but it may be moved to strike out A C or A C D, or D B, or C D B.

117. *When it is proposed to amend by inserting a paragraph, this amendment may be amended in three different ways, namely, either by striking out a part of the paragraph; or by inserting something into it; or by striking out and inserting.*

118. Thus, if it is proposed to amend A B by inserting C D, this amendment may be

---

[1] This is the common case of striking out a paragraph, after having amended it by inserting words.

amended either by striking out C or D, or inserting E, or by striking out C or D and inserting E.

119. When it is proposed to amend by inserting a paragraph, those who are in favor of the amendment should amend it, if necessary, before the question is taken; because if it is rejected, it cannot be moved again, and, if received, it cannot be amended.

120. There is no precedence of one over another in amendments to amendments by inserting, any more than in amendments to amendments by striking out.

121. On a motion to amend by inserting a paragraph, the manner of stating the question is, first, to read the passage to be amended, as it stands; then the words proposed to be inserted; and, lastly, the whole passage as it will stand if the amendment prevails.

Sect. VIII. Amendments by striking out and inserting.

122. The third form of amending a proposition, namely, by striking out certain words and inserting others in their place, is, in fact, a combination of the other two forms; and may

accordingly be divided into those two forms, either by a vote of the assembly, or on the demand of a member, under a special rule to that effect[1]. [¶ 323.]

123. If the motion is divided, the question is first to be taken on striking out; and if that is decided in the affirmative, then, on inserting; but if the former is decided in the negative, the latter falls, of course. On a division, the proceedings are the same, in reference to each branch of the question, beginning with the striking out, as if each branch had been moved by itself.

124. If the motion to strike out and insert is put to the question undivided, and is decided in the negative, the same motion cannot be made again; but, it may be moved to strike out the same words, and, 1, insert nothing; 2, insert other words; 3, insert the same words with others; 4, insert a part of the same words with others; 5, strike out the same words with others, and insert the same; 6, strike out a

---

[1] Mr. Jefferson (§ xxxv.) says, " the question, if desired, is then to be divided," &c.; but, as he makes no exception of a motion to strike out and insert, when treating of the subject of division, and does not here state it as an exception, he undoubtedly supposes the division in this case to be made in the regular and usual manner.

part of the same words with others, and insert the same; 7, strike out other words and insert the same; and, 8, insert the same words, without striking out any thing.

125. If the motion to strike out and insert is decided in the affirmative, it cannot be then moved to insert the words struck out or a part of them, or to strike out the words inserted, or a part of them; but, it may be moved, 1, to insert the same words with others; 2, to insert a part of the same words with others; 3, to strike out the same words with others; or, 4, to strike out a part of the same words with others.

126. When it is proposed to amend by striking out and inserting, this amendment may be amended in three different ways in the paragraph proposed to be struck out, and also in the paragraph proposed to be inserted, namely, by striking out, or inserting, or striking out and inserting. And those who are in favor of either paragraph must amend it, before the question is taken, for the reasons already stated, namely, that, if decided in the affirmative, the part struck out cannot be restored, nor can the part inserted be amended; and, if decided in the negative, the part proposed to be struck out cannot be amended, nor can the

paragraph proposed to be inserted be moved again.

127. On a motion to amend, by striking out certain words and inserting others, the manner of stating the question is first to read the whole passage to be amended, as it stands; then the words proposed to be struck out; next those to be inserted; and, lastly, the whole passage as it will stand when amended.

SECT. IX. AMENDMENTS CHANGING THE NATURE OF A QUESTION.

128. The term amendment is in strictness applicable only to those changes of a proposition, by which it is improved, that is, rendered more effectual for the purpose which it has in view, or made to express more clearly and definitely the sense which it is intended to express. Hence it seems proper, that those only should undertake to amend a proposition, who are friendly to it; but this is by no means the rule; when a proposition is regularly moved and seconded, it is in the possession of the assembly, and cannot be withdrawn but by its leave; it has then become the basis of the future proceedings of the assembly, and may be put into

any shape, and turned to any purpose, that the assembly may think proper.

129. It is consequently allowable to amend a proposition in such a manner as entirely to alter its nature, and to make it bear a sense different from what it was originally intended to bear; so that the friends of it, as it was first introduced, may themselves be forced to vote against it, in its amended form.

130. This mode of proceeding is sometimes adopted for the purpose of defeating a proposition, by compelling its original friends to unite with those who are opposed to it, in voting for its rejection. Thus, in the British house of commons, Jan. 29, 1765, a resolution being moved, "That a general warrant for apprehending the authors, printers, or publishers of a libel, together with their papers, is not warranted by law, and is an high violation of the liberty of the subject:" — it was moved to amend this motion by prefixing the following paragraph, namely: "That in the particular case of libels, it is proper and necessary to fix, by a vote of this house only, what ought to be deemed the law in respect of general warrants; and, for that purpose, at the time when the determination of the legality of such warrants,

in the instance of a most seditious and treasonable libel, is actually depending before the courts of law, for this house to declare "—*that a general warrant for apprehending the authors, printers, or publishers of a libel, together with their papers, is not warranted by law, and is an high violation of the liberty of the subject.* The amendment was adopted, after a long debate, and then the resolution as amended was immediately rejected without a division[1].

131. But sometimes the nature of a proposition is changed by means of amendments, with a view to its adoption in a sense the very opposite of what it was originally intended to bear. The following is a striking example of this mode of proceeding. In the house of commons, April 10, 1744, a resolution was moved, declaring, "That the issuing and paying to the Duke of Aremberg the sum of forty thousand pounds sterling, to put the

---

1 This mode of defeating a measure, however, is not always successful. In 1780, Mr. Dunning having made a motion, in the house of commons, "that, in the opinion of this house, the influence of the crown has increased, is increasing, and ought to be diminished," Dundas, lord-advocate of Scotland, in order to defeat the motion, proposed to amend, by inserting, after the words, *in the opinion of this house*, the words, *it is now necessary to declare that*, &c. But this amendment, instead of intimidating the friends of the original motion was at once adopted by them, and the resolution passed as amended.

Austrian troops in motion in the year 1742, was a dangerous misapplication of public money, and destructive of the rights of parliament." The object of this resolution was to censure the conduct of the ministers; and the friends of the ministry, being in a majority, might have voted directly upon the motion and rejected it. But they preferred to turn it into a resolution approving of the conduct of ministers on the occasion referred to; and it was accordingly moved to amend, by leaving out the words "a dangerous misapplication," &c to the end of the motion, and inserting instead thereof the words, "necessary for putting the said troops in motion, and of great consequence to the common cause." The amendment being adopted, it was resolved (reversing the original proposition) "That the issuing and paying to the Duke of Aremberg the sum of forty thousand pounds, to put the Austrian troops in motion, in the year 1742, was necessary for putting the said troops in motion, and of great consequence to the common cause."

132. It is a mode of defeating a proposition, somewhat similar to that above mentioned, to carry out or extend the principle of it, by means of amendments, so as to show the

inconvenience, absurdity, or danger of its adoption, with such evident clearness, that it becomes impossible for the assembly to agree to it. Thus, a motion having been made in the house of commons, "for copies of all the letters written by the lords of the admiralty to a certain officer in the navy," it was moved to amend the motion by adding these words;—"which letters may contain orders, or be relative to orders, not executed, and still subsisting." This amendment being adopted, the motion as amended was unanimously rejected.

133. It will be seen, from the foregoing examples, that as the mover of a proposition is under no restriction as to embracing incongruous matters under the same motion; so, on the other hand, the assembly may engraft upon a motion, by way of amendment, matter which is not only incongruous with, but entirely opposed to, the motion as originally introduced; and, in legislative assemblies, it is not unusual to amend a bill by striking out all after the enacting clause, and inserting an entirely new bill; or to amend a resolution by striking out all after the words "Resolved that," and inserting a proposition of a wholly different tenor. [¶ 324.]

CHAPTER X.

OF THE ORDER AND SUCCESSION OF QUESTIONS.

134. It is a general rule, that, when a proposition is regularly before a deliberative assembly, for its consideration, no other proposition or motion can regularly be made or arise, so as to take the place of the former, and be first acted upon, unless it be either, *first*, a privileged question; *secondly*, a subsidiary question; or, *thirdly*, an incidental question or motion.

135. All these motions take the place of the principal motion, or main question, as it is usually called, and are to be first put to the question; and, among themselves, also, there are some, which, in like manner, take the place of all the others. Some of these questions merely supersede the principal question, until they have been decided; and, when decided, whether affirmatively or negatively, leave that question as before. Others of them also supersede the principal question, until they are decided; and, when decided one way, dispose of the principal question; but, if decided the other way, leave it as before.

SECT. I. PRIVILEGED QUESTIONS.

136. There are certain motions or questions, which, on account of the superior importance attributed to them, either in consequence of a vote of the assembly, or in themselves considered, or of the necessity of the proceedings to which they lead, are entitled to take the place of any other subject or proposition, which may then be under consideration, and to be first acted upon and decided by the assembly. These are called privileged questions, because they are entitled to precedence over other questions, though they are of different degrees among themselves. Questions of this nature are of three kinds, namely, *first*, motions to adjourn; *secondly*, motions or questions relating to the rights and privileges of the assembly, or of its members individually; and, *thirdly*, motions for the orders of the day.

ADJOURNMENT.

137. A motion to adjourn takes the place of all other questions whatsoever[1]; for, other-

---

[1] It is commonly said, that a motion to adjourn is always in order, but this is not precisely true. The question of adjournment may,

wise, the assembly might be kept sitting against its will, and for an indefinite time; but, in order to entitle this motion to precedence, it must be simply to "adjourn," without the addition of any particular day or time. And, as the object of this motion, when made in the midst of some other proceeding, and with a view to supersede a question already proposed, is simply to break up the sitting, it does not admit of any amendment by the addition of a particular day, or in any other manner; though, if a motion to adjourn is made, when no other business is before the assembly, it may be amended like other questions. [¶ 325.]

138. A motion to adjourn is merely, "that this assembly do now adjourn;" and, if it is carried in the affirmative, the assembly is adjourned to the next sitting day; unless it has previously come to a resolution, that, on rising, it will adjourn to a particular day; in which case, it is adjourned to that day.

---

indeed, be moved repeatedly on the same day; yet, in strictness, not without some intermediate question being proposed, after one motion to adjourn is disposed of, and before the next motion is made for adjourning; as, for example, an amendment to a pending question, or for the reading of some paper. The reason of this is, that, until some other proceeding has intervened, the question already decided is the same as that newly moved.

139. An adjournment without day, that is, without any time being fixed for reassembling, would, in the case of any other than a legislative assembly, be equivalent to a dissolution[1]

140. When a question is interrupted by an adjournment, before any vote or question has been taken upon it, it is thereby removed from before the assembly, and will not stand before it, as a matter of course, at its next meeting, but must be brought forward in the usual way.

Questions of Privilege.

141 The questions, next in relative importance, and which supersede all others for the time being, except that of adjournment, are those which concern the rights and privileges of the assembly, or of its individual members; as, for example, when the proceedings of the assembly are disturbed or interrupted, whether by strangers or members; or where a quarrel arises between two members; and, in these cases, the matter of privilege supersedes the question pending at the time, together with all

---

[1] It is quite common, when the business of a deliberative assembly has been brought to a close, *to adjourn* the assembly *without day.* A better form is to *dissolve it;* as an adjournment without day if we regard the etymology of the word *adjourn*, is a contradiction in terms.

subsidiary and incidental ones, and must be first disposed of. When settled, the question interrupted by it is to be resumed, at the point where it was suspended.

Orders of the Day.

142. When the consideration of a subject has been assigned for a particular day, by an order of the assembly, the matter so assigned is called the order of the day for that day. If, in the course of business, as commonly happens in legislative assemblies, there are several subjects assigned for the same day, they are called the orders of the day.

143. A question, which is thus made the subject of an order for its consideration on a particular day, is thereby made a privileged question for that day; the order being a repeal, as to this special case, of the general rule as to business. If, therefore, any other proposition (with the exception of the two preceding) is moved, or arises, on the day assigned for the consideration of a particular subject, a motion for the order of the day will supersede the question first made, together with all subsidiary and incidental questions connected with it, and must be first put and decided; for if the

debate or consideration of that subject were allowed to proceed, it might continue through the day and thus defeat the order.

144. But this motion, to entitle it to precedence, must be for the orders generally, if there is more than one, and not for any particular one; and, if decided in the affirmative, that is, that the assembly will now proceed to the orders of the day, they must then be read and gone through with, in the order in which they stand; priority of order being considered to give priority of right.

145. If the consideration of a subject is assigned for a particular hour on the day named, a motion to proceed to it is not a privileged motion, until that hour has arrived; but, if no hour is fixed, the order is for the entire day and every part of it.

146. Where there are several orders of the day, and one of them is fixed for a particular hour, if the orders are taken up before that hour, they are to be proceeded with as they stand, until that hour, and then the subject assigned for that hour is the next in order; but, if the orders are taken up at that time or afterwards, that particular subject must be considered as the first in order.

147. If the motion for the orders of the day is decided in the affirmative, the original question is removed from before the assembly, in the same manner as if it had been interrupted by an adjournment, and does not stand before the assembly, as a matter of course, at its next meeting, but must be renewed in the usual way.

148. If the motion is decided in the negative, the vote of the assembly is a discharge of the orders, so far as they interfere with the consideration of the subject then before it, and entitles that subject to be first disposed of.

149. Orders of the day, unless proceeded in and disposed of on the day assigned, fall, of course, and must be renewed for some other day. It may be provided, however, by a special rule, as in the legislative assemblies of Massachusetts, that the orders for a particular day shall hold for every succeeding day, until disposed of.

SECT. II. INCIDENTAL QUESTIONS.

150. Incidental questions are such as arise out of other questions, and are consequently to be decided before the questions which give

rise to them. Of this nature are, *first*, questions of order; *second*, motions for the reading of papers, &c.; *third*, leave to withdraw a motion; *fourth*, suspension of a rule; and, *fifth*, amendment of an amendment.

Questions of Order.

151. It is the duty of the presiding officer of a deliberative assembly, to enforce the rules and orders of the body over which he presides, in all its proceedings; and this without question, debate, or delay, in all cases, in which the breach of order, or the departure from rule, is manifest. It is also the right of every member, taking notice of the breach of a rule, to insist upon the enforcement of it in the same manner.

152. But, though no question can be made, as to the enforcement of the rules, when there is a breach or manifest departure from them, so long as any member insists upon their enforcement; yet questions may and do frequently arise, as to the fact of there being a breach of order, or a violation of the rules in a particular proceeding; and these questions must be decided before a case can arise for the enforcement of the rules. Questions of

this kind are denominated questions of order.

153. When any question of this nature arises, in the course of any other proceeding, it necessarily supersedes the further consideration of the subject out of which it arises, until that question is disposed of; then the original motion or proceeding revives, and resumes its former position, unless it has been itself disposed of by the question of order.

154. When a question of order is raised, as it may be by any one member, it is not stated from the chair, and decided by the assembly, like other questions; but is decided, in the first instance, by the presiding officer, without any previous debate or discussion by the assembly. If the decision of the presiding officer is not satisfactory, any one member may object to it, and have the question decided by the assembly. This is called *appealing* from the decision of the chair. The question is then stated by the presiding officer, on the appeal, namely: *shall the decision of the chair stand as the decision of the assembly?* and it is thereupon debated and decided by the assembly, in the same manner as any other question; except that the presiding

officer is allowed to take a part in the debate, which, on ordinary occasions, he is prohibited from doing. [¶ 326.]

READING PAPERS.

155. It is, for obvious reasons, a general rule, that, where papers are laid before a deliberative assembly, for its action, every member has a right to have them once read at the table, before he can be compelled to vote on them; and, consequently, when the reading of any paper, relative to a question before the assembly, is called for under this rule, no question need be made as to the reading; the paper is read by the clerk, under the direction of the presiding officer, as a matter of course.

156. But, with the exception of papers coming under this rule, it is not the right of any member to read himself, or to have read, any paper, book, or document whatever, without the leave of the assembly, upon a motion made and a question put for the purpose. The delay and interruption, which would otherwise ensue from reading every paper that might be called for, show the absolute necessity of restricting the rule within the narrowest

possible limits, consistently with permitting every member to have as much information as possible, on the subjects in reference to which he is about to vote.

157. When, therefore, a member desires that any paper, book, or document, on the table, whether printed or written (except as above mentioned) should be read for his own information, or that of the assembly; or desires to read any such paper, book, or document, in his place, in the course of a debate, or otherwise; or even to read his own speech, which he has prepared beforehand and committed to writing; in all these cases, if any objection is made, he must obtain leave of the assembly, for the reading, by a motion and vote for the purpose

158. When the reading of a paper is evidently for information, and not for delay, it is the usual practice for the presiding officer to allow of it, unless objection is made, in which case leave must be asked; and this is seldom refused, where there is no intentional or gross abuse of the time and patience of the assembly.

159. It is not now the practice, as it once was, in legislative assemblies, to read all

papers that are presented, especially when they are referred to committees immediately on their presentation; though the right of every member to insist upon one reading is still admitted. It would be impossible, with the amount of business done by legislative bodies, at the present day, to devote much of their time to the reading of papers.

160. When, in the course of a debate or other proceeding, the reading of a paper is called for, and a question is made upon it, this question is incidental to the former, and must be first decided.

Withdrawal of a Motion.

161. A motion, when regularly made, seconded, and proposed from the chair, is then in the possession of the assembly, and cannot be withdrawn by the mover, or directly disposed of in any manner, but by a vote; hence, if the mover of a question wishes to modify it, or to substitute a different one in its place, he must obtain the leave of the assembly for that purpose; which leave can only be had, if objection is made, by a motion and question in the usual mode of proceeding. [¶ 327.]

162. If this motion is decided in the affirmative, the motion to which it relates is thereby removed from before the assembly, as if it had never been moved; if in the negative, the business proceeds as before.

SUSPENSION OF A RULE.

163. When any contemplated motion or proceeding is rendered impracticable, by reason of the existence of some special rule by which it is prohibited, it has become an established practice in this country, to suspend or dispense with the rule, for the purpose of admitting the proceeding or motion which is desired. This can only be done by a motion and question; and, where this course is taken in order to a motion having reference to a proposition then under consideration, a motion to suspend the rule supersedes the original question for the time being, and is first to be decided.

164. It is usual, in the code of rules adopted by deliberative assemblies, and especially legislative bodies, to provide that a certain number exceeding a majority, as two thirds or three fourths, shall be competent to the suspension of a rule in a particular case; where this is not provided, there seems to be no

other mode of suspending or dispensing with a rul϶ than by general consent.

Amendment of Amendments.

165. In treating of amendments, it has already been seen, that it is allowable to amend a proposed amendment; and that the question on such sub-amendment must necessarily be put and decided before putting the question on the amendment. The former is incidental to the latter, and supersedes it for the time being.

Sect. III. Subsidiary Questions.

166. Subsidiary, or secondary, questions or motions, as has already been stated, are those which relate to a principal motion, and are made use of to enable the assembly to dispose of it in the most appropriate manner. These motions have the effect to supersede, and, in some cases, when decided one way, to dispose of, the principal question. They are also of different degrees among themselves, and, according to their several natures, supersede, and sometimes dispose of, one another.

167 The subsidiary motions in common use are the fol'owing, namely:—lie on the table,—

the previous question, — postponement, either indefinite or to a day certain, — commitment, — and, amendment.

168. It is a general rule, with certain exceptions which will be immediately mentioned, that subsidiary motions cannot be applied to one another; as, for example, suppose a motion to postpone, commit, or amend a principal question, it cannot be moved to suppress the motion to postpone, &c., by putting a previous question on it; or, suppose the previous question is moved, or a commitment, or amendment, of a main question, it cannot be moved to postpone the previous question, or the motion for commitment or amendment. The reasons for this rule are: 1. It would be absurd to separate the appendage from its principal; 2. It would be a piling of questions one on another, which, to avoid embarrassment, is not allowed; and, 3. The same result may be reached more simply by voting against the motion which it is attempted to dispose of by another secondary motion.

169. The exceptions to the rule above stated are, that motions to postpone (either to a day certain or indefinitely), to commit, or to amend, a principal question, may be

amended for the reason, that "the useful character of amendment gives it a privilege of attaching itself to a secondary and privileged motion"; that is, a subsidiary motion to carry out and improve another may be applied to that other, but a subsidiary motion to dispose of or suppress another is not admissible. Hence, the subsidiary motions above mentioned may be amended.

170. A previous question, however, cannot be amended; the nature of it not admitting of any change. Parliamentary usage has fixed its form to be, shall the main question be now put? that is, at this instant; and, as the present instant is but one, it cannot admit of any modification; and to change it to the next day or any other moment is without example or utility. For the same reasons, also, that the form of it is fixed by parliamentary usage, and is already as simple as it can be, a motion to lie on the table cannot be amended.

Lie on the Table.

171. This motion is usually resorted to, when the assembly has something else before it, which claims its present attention, and therefore desires to lay aside a proposition for

a short but indefinite time, reserving to itself the power to take it up when convenient. This motion takes precedence of and supersedes all the other subsidiary motions.

172. If decided in the affirmative, the principal motion, together with all the other motions, subsidiary and incidental, connected with it, is removed from before the assembly, until it is again taken up; which it may be, by motion and vote, at any time, when the assembly pleases.

173. If decided in the negative, the business proceeds in the same manner as if the motion had never been made.

Previous Question.

174. This motion has already been described (63), and the nature and effect of it fully stated. It stands in an equal degree with all the other subsidiary motions, except the motion to lie on the table; and, consequently, if first moved, is not subject to be superseded by a motion to postpone, commit, or amend.

175. If the previous question is moved before the others above mentioned, and put to the question, it has the effect to prevent those motions from being made at all; for,

if decided affirmatively, to wit, that the main question shall now be put, it would of course be contrary to the decision of the assembly, and therefore against order, to postpone, commit, or amend; and if decided negatively, to wit, that the main question shall not now be put, this takes the main question out of the possession of the assembly, for the day, so that there is then nothing before it to postpone, commit, or amend[1].

Postponement.

176. The motion to postpone is either indefinite, or to a day certain; and, in both these forms, may be amended; in the former, by making it to a day certain, — in the latter, by substituting one day for another. But, in the latter case, propositions to substitute different days for that originally named, bear more resemblance to propositions for filling blanks, than they do to amendments, and should be considered and treated accordingly.

---

[1] In the house of representatives of Massachusetts, as the effect of a negative decision of the previous question is not to remove the principal question from before the house, that question is still open to postponement, commitment, or amendment, notwithstanding such negative decision.

177. If, therefore, a motion is made for an indefinite postponement, it may be moved to amend the motion, by making it to a day certain. If any other day is desired, it may be moved as an amendment to the amendment; or it may be moved as an independent motion, when the amendment has been re jected.

178. If a motion is made for a postponement to a day certain, it may be amended by the substitution of a different day; but in this case, a more simple and effectual mode of proceeding is to consider the day as a blank, to be filled in the usual manner, beginning with the longest time.

179. This motion stands in the same degree with motions for the previous question, — to commit, — and to amend; and, if first made, is not susceptible of being superseded by them.

180. If a motion for postponement is decided affirmatively, the proposition to which it is applied is removed from before the assembly, with all its appendages and incidents, and consequently there is no ground for either of the other subsidiary motions; if decided nega-

tively, that the proposition shall not be postponed, that question may then be suppressed by the previous question, or committed, or amended.

Commitment.

181. A motion to commit, or recommit (which is the term used when the proposition has already been once committed), may be amended, by the substitution of one kind of committee for another, or by enlarging or diminishing the number of the members of the committee, as originally proposed, or by instructions to the committee.

182. This motion stands in the same degree with the previous question and postponement — and, if first made, is not superseded by them — but it takes precedence of a motion to amend.

183. If decided affirmatively, the proposition is removed from before the assembly; and, consequently, there is no ground for the previous question, or for postponement, or amendment; if negatively, to wit, that the principal question shall not be committed, that question may then be suppressed by the previous question, or postponed, or amended.

AMENDMENT.

184. A motion to amend, as has been seen, may be itself amended. It stands in the same degree only with the previous question and indefinite postponement, and neither, if first moved, is superseded by the other.

185. But this motion is liable to be superseded by a motion to postpone to a day certain; so that amendment and postponement competing, the latter is to be first put. The reason is, that a question for amendment is not suppressed by postponing or adjourning the principal question, but remains before the assembly, whenever the main question is resumed; for otherwise, it might happen, that the occasion for other urgent business might go by and be lost by length of debate on the amendment, if the assembly had no power to postpone the whole subject.

186. A motion to amend may also be superseded by a motion to commit; so that the latter, though subsequently moved, is to be first put; because, "in truth, it facilitates and befriends the motion to amend."

187. The effect of both a negative and an affirmative decision of amendments has already been considered (94 to 127)

CHAPTER XI.

OF THE ORDER OF PROCEEDING.

188. When several subjects are before the assembly, that is, on their table for consideration (for there can be but a single subject *under* consideration at the same time), and no priority has been given to any one over another, the presiding officer is not precisely bound to any order, as to what matters shall be first taken up; but is left to his own discretion, unless the assembly on a question decide to take up a particular subject.

189. A settled order of business, however, where the proceedings of an assembly are likely to last a considerable time, and the matters before it are somewhat numerous, is useful if not necessary for the government of the presiding officer, and to restrain individual members from calling up favorite measures, or matters under their special charge, out of their just time. It is also desirable, for directing the discretion of the assembly, when a motion is made to take up a particular matter, to the prejudice of others, which are of right

entitled to be first attended to, in the general order of business.

190. The order of business may be established in virtue of some general rule, or by special orders relating to each particular subject; and must, of course, necessarily depend upon the nature and amount of the matters before the assembly.

191. The natural order, in considering and amending any paper, which consists of several distinct propositions, is, to begin at the beginning, and proceed through it by paragraphs; and this order of proceeding, if strictly adhered to, as it should always be in numerous assemblies, would prevent any amendment in a former part, from being admissible, after a latter part had been amended; but this rule does not seem to be so essential to be observed in smaller bodies, in which it may often be advantageous to allow of going from one part of a paper to another, for the purpose of amendments.

192. To this natural order of beginning at the beginning, there is one exception according to parliamentary usage, where a resolution or series of resolutions, or other paper, has a preamble or title; in which case, the preamble

or title is postponed, until the residue of the paper is gone through with.

193. In considering a proposition consisting of several paragraphs, the course is, for the whole paper to be read entirely through, in the first place, by the clerk; then, a second time, by the presiding officer, by paragraphs; pausing at the end of each, and putting questions for amending, if amendments are proposed; and, when the whole paper has been gone through with, in this manner, the presiding officer puts the final question on agreeing to or adopting the whole paper, as amended, or unamended.

194. When a paper, which has been referred to a committee, and reported back to the assembly, is taken up for consideration, the amendments only are first read, in course, by the clerk. The presiding officer then reads the first, and puts it to the question, and so on until the whole are adopted or rejected, before any other amendment is admitted, with the exception of an amendment to an amendment. When the amendments reported by the committee have been thus disposed of, the presiding officer pauses, and gives time for amendments to be proposed in the assembly

to the body of the paper (which he also does, if the paper has been reported without amendments, putting no questions but on amendments proposed); and when through the whole, he puts the question on agreeing to or adopting the paper, as the resolution, order, &c., of the assembly.

195. The final question is sometimes stated merely on the acceptance of the report, but a better form is on agreeing with the committee in the resolution, order, or whatever else the conclusion of the report may be, as amended, or without amendment; and the resolution or order is then to be entered in the journal as the resolution, &c., of the assembly, and not as the report of the committee accepted.

196. When the paper referred to a committee is reported back, as amended, in a new draft (which may be and often is done, where the amendments are numerous and comparatively unimportant), the new draft is to be considered as an amendment, and is to be first amended, if necessary, and then put to the question as an amendment reported by the committee; or, the course may be, first to accept the new draft, as a substitute for the original paper, and then to treat it as such.

197. It often happens, that, besides a principal question, there are several others connected with it, pending at the same time, which are to be taken in their order; as, for example, suppose, *first*, a principal motion; *second*, a motion to amend; *third*, a motion to commit; *fourth*, the preceding motions being pending, a question of order arises in the debate, which gives occasion, *fifth*, to a question of privilege, and this leads, *sixth*, to a subsidiary motion, as, to lie on the table. The regular course of proceeding requires the motion to lie on the table to be first put; if this is negatived, the question of privilege is then settled; after that comes the question of order; then the question of commitment; if that is negatived, the question of amendment is taken; and, lastly, the main question. This example will sufficiently illustrate the manner in which questions may grow out of one another, and in what order they are to be decided[1].

198. When a motion is made and seconded, it is the duty of the presiding officer to propose

---

[1] The order of motions, for the disposal of any question, is usually fixed by a special rule, in legislative assemblies. See note to paragraph 61.

it to the assembly; until this is done, it is not a question before the assembly, to be acted upon or considered in any manner; and consequently it is not then in order for any member to rise either to debate it, or to make any motion in relation to it whatever.

199. It is therefore a most unparliamentary and abusive proceeding to allow a principal motion and a subsidiary one relating to it to be proposed and stated together, and to be put to the question in their order; as is done, when a member moves a principal question, a resolution, for example, and, at the same time, the previous question, or that the resolution lie on the table. In such a case, the presiding officer should take no notice whatever of the subsidiary motion, but should propose the principal one by itself in the usual manner, before allowing any other to be made. Other members, then, would not be deprived of their rights of debate, &c., in relation to the subject moved.

200. When a member has obtained the floor, he cannot be cut off from addressing the assembly, on the question before it; nor, when speaking, can he be interrupted in his speech, by any other member rising and moving an

adjournment, or for the orders of the day, or by making any other privileged motion of the same kind; it being a general rule, that a member in possession of the floor, or proceeding with his speech, cannot be taken down or interrupted, but by a call to order; and the question of order being decided, he is still to be heard through. A call for an adjournment, or for the orders of the day, or for the question, by gentlemen in their seats, is not a motion; as no motion can be made, without rising and addressing the chair, and being called to by the presiding officer. Such calls for the question are themselves breaches of order, which, though the member who has risen may respect them, as an expression of the impatience of the assembly at further debate, do not prevent him from going on if he pleases. [¶ 328.]

CHAPTER XII.

OF ORDER IN DEBATE.

201. Debate in a deliberative assembly must be distinguished from forensic debate, or that which takes place before a judicial tribunal; the former being, in theory, at least, more the expression of individual opinions among the members of the same body; the latter more a contest for victory, between the disputants, before a distinct and independent body; the former not admitting of replies; the latter regarding reply as the right of one of the parties[1].

202. It is a general rule, in all deliberative assemblies, that the presiding officer shall not participate in the debate, or other proceedings, in any other capacity than as such officer. He is only allowed, therefore, to state matters

[1] An exception to this rule is sometimes made in favor of the mover of a question, who is allowed, at the close of the debate, to reply to the arguments brought against his motion; but this is a matter of favor and indulgence, and not of right.

of fact within his knowledge; to inform the assembly on points of order or the course of proceeding, when called upon for that purpose, or when he finds it necessary to do so; and, on appeals from his decision on questions of order, to address the assembly in debate.

SECT. I. AS TO THE MANNER OF SPEAKING.

203. When a member desires to address the assembly, on any subject before it (as well as to make a motion), he is to rise and stand up in his place, uncovered, and to address himself not to the assembly, or any particular member, but to the presiding officer, who, on hearing him, calls to him by his name, that the assembly may take notice who it is that speaks, and give their attention accordingly. If any question arises, as to who shall be entitled to the floor, where several members rise at or nearly at the same time, it is decided in the manner already described (46), as to obtaining the floor to make a motion.

204. It is customary, indeed, for the presiding officer, after a motion has been made, seconded, and proposed, to give the floor to

the mover[1], in preference to others, if he rises to speak; or, on resuming a debate, after an adjournment, to give the floor, if he desires it, to the mover of the adjournment, in preference to other members; or, where two or more members claim the floor, to prefer him who is opposed to the measure in question; but, in all these cases, the determination of the presiding officer may be overruled by the assembly.

205. It is sometimes thought, that, when a member, in the course of debate, breaks off his speech, and gives up the floor to another for a particular purpose, he is entitled to it again, as of right, when that purpose is accomplished; but, though this is generally conceded, yet, when a member gives up the floor for one purpose, he does so for all; and it is not possible for the presiding officer to take notice of and enforce agreements of this nature between members.

206. No person, in speaking, is to mention

---

[1] Sometimes a member, instead of proposing his motion, at first, proceeds with his speech; but, in such a case, he is liable to be taken down to order, unless he states that he intends to conclude with a motion, and informs the assembly what that motion is, and then he may be allowed to proceed.

a member then present by his name; but to describe him by his seat in the assembly, or as the member who spoke last, or last but one, or on the other side of the question, or by some other equivalent expression. The purpose of this rule is to guard as much as possible against the excitement of all personal feeling, either of favor or of hostility, by separating, as it were, the official from the personal character of each member, and having regard to the former only in the debate.

207. If the presiding officer rises up to speak, any other member, who may have risen for the same purpose, ought to sit down, in order that the former may be first heard; but this rule does not authorize the presiding officer to interrupt a member, whilst speaking, or to cut off one to whom he has given the floor; he must wait like other members, until such member has done speaking. [¶ 329.]

208. A member, whilst speaking, must remain standing in his place, uncovered; and, when he has finished his speech, he ought to resume his seat; but if unable to stand without pain or inconvenience, in consequence of age, sickness, or other infirmity, he may be indulged to speak sitting.

SECT. II. AS TO THE MATTER IN SPEAKING.

209 Every question, that can be made in a deliberative assembly, is susceptible of being debated[1], according to its nature; that is, every member has the right of expressing his opinion upon it. Hence, it is a general rule, and the principal one relating to this matter, that, in debate, those who speak are to confine themselves to the question, and not to speak impertinently, or beside the subject. So long as a member has the floor, and keeps within the rule, he may speak for as long a time as he pleases; though, if an uninteresting speaker trespasses too much upon the time and patience of the assembly, the members seldom fail to show their dissatisfaction, in some way or other, which induces him to bring his remarks to a close. [¶ 330.]

210. It is also a rule, that no person, in speaking, is to use indecent language against the proceedings of the assembly, or to reflect upon any of its prior determinations, unless he means to conclude his remarks with a

[1] In legislative bodies, it is usual to provide, that certain questions, as, for example, to adjourn, to lie on the table, for the previous question, or, as to the order of business, shall be decided without debate

motion to rescind such determination; but while a proposition under consideration is still pending, and not adopted, though it may have been reported by a committee, reflections on it are no reflections on the assembly. The rule applies equally to the proceedings of committees; which are, indeed, the proceedings of the assembly.

211. Another rule in speaking is, that no member is at liberty to digress from the matter of the question, to fall upon the person of another, and to speak reviling, nipping, or unmannerly words of or to him. The nature or consequences of a measure may be reprobated in strong terms; but to arraign the motives of those who advocate it, is a personality and against order.

212. It is very often an extremely difficult and delicate matter to decide whether the remarks of a member are pertinent or relevant to the question; but it will, in general, be safe for the presiding officer to consider them so, unless they very clearly reflect, in an improper manner, either upon the person or motives of a member, or upon the proceedings of the assembly; or the member speaking digresses from or manifestly mistakes the question.

8

213. It often happens in the consideration of a subject, that, whilst the general question remains the same, the particular question before the assembly is constantly changing; thus, while, for example, the general question is on the adoption of a series of resolutions, the particular question may, at one moment, be on an amendment; at another on postponement; and, again, on the previous question. In all these cases, the particular question supersedes, for the time, the main question; and those who speak to it must confine their remarks accordingly. The enforcement of order, in this respect, requires the closest attention on the part of the presiding officer. [¶ 331.]

214. When a member is interrupted by the presiding officer, or called to order by a member, for irrelevancy or departing from the question, a question may be made as to whether he shall be allowed to proceed in his remarks, in the manner he was speaking when he was interrupted; but, if no question is made, or if one is made and decided in the negative, he is still to be allowed to proceed in order, that is, abandoning the objectionable course of remark.

SECT. III. AS TO TIMES OF SPEAKING.

215. The general rule, in all deliberative assemblies, unless it is otherwise specially provided, is, that no member shall speak more than once to the same question[1]; although the debate on that question may be adjourned and continued through several days; and, although a member, who desires to speak a second time, has, in the course of the debate, changed his opinion.

216. This rule refers to the same question, technically considered; for, if a resolution is moved and debated, and then referred to a committee, those who speak on the introduction of the motion may speak again on the question presented by the report of the committee, though it is substantially the same question with the former; and, so, members, who have spoken on the principal or main question, may speak again on all the subsidiary or incidental questions arising in the course of the debate. [¶ 332.]

---

[1] The mover and seconder, if they do not speak to the question, at the time when the motion is made and seconded, have the same right with other members to address the assembly.

217. The rule, as to speaking but once on a question, if strictly enforced, will prevent a member from speaking a second time, without the general consent of the assembly, so long as there is any other member who himself desires to speak; but, when all who desire to speak have spoken, a member may speak a second time by leave of the assembly.

218. A member may also be permitted to speak a second time, in the same debate, in order to clear a matter of fact; or merely to explain himself in some material part of his speech; or to the orders of the assembly, if they be transgressed (although no question may be made), but carefully keeping within that line, and not falling into the matter itself. [¶ 333.]

219. It is sometimes supposed, that, because a member has a right to explain himself, he therefore has a right to interrupt another member, whilst speaking, in order to make the explanation: but this is a mistake; he should wait until the member speaking has finished; and if a member, on being requested, yields the floor for an explanation, he relinquishes it altogether.

SECT. IV. AS TO STOPPING DEBATE.

220. The only mode in use, in this country, until recently, for the purpose of putting an end to an unprofitable or tiresome debate, was by moving the previous question; the effect of which motion, as already explained, if decided in the affirmative, is to require the main or principal question to be immediately taken. When this question is moved, therefore, it necessarily suspends all further consideration of the main question, and precludes all further debate or amendment of it; though, as has been seen, it stands in the same degree with postponement, amendment, and commitment; and, unless in virtue of a special rule, cannot be moved while either of those motions is pending.

221. The other mode of putting an end to debate, which has recently been introduced into use, is for the assembly to adopt beforehand a special order in reference to a particular subject, that, at such a time specified, all debate upon it shall cease, and all motions or questions pending in relation to it shall be decided.

222. Another rule, which has lately been introduced for the purpose of shortening rather than stopping debate, is, that no member shall be permitted to speak more than a certain specified time on any question; so that, when the time allotted has expired, the presiding officer announces the fact, and the member speaking resumes his seat.

Sect. V. As to Decorum in Debate.

223. Every member having the right to be heard, every other member is bound to conduct himself in such a manner, that this right may be effectual. Hence, it is a rule of order, as well as of decency, that no member is to disturb another in his speech by hissing, coughing, spitting; by speaking, or whispering; by passing between the presiding officer and the member speaking; by going across the assembly-room, or walking up and down in it; or by any other disorderly deportment, which tends to disturb or disconcert a member who is speaking.

224. But, if a member speaking finds, that he is not regarded with that respectful attention, which his equal right demands, — that

it is not the inclination of the assembly to hear him, — and that by conversation or any other noise they endeavor to drown his voice, — it is his most prudent course to submit himself to the pleasure of the assembly, and to sit down; for it scarcely ever happens, that the members of an assembly are guilty of this piece of ill manners, without some excuse or provocation, or that they are so wholly inattentive to one, who says any thing worth their hearing.

225. It is the duty of the presiding officer, in such a case, to endeavor to reduce the assembly to order and decorum; but, if his repeated calls to order, and his appeals to the good sense and decency of the members, prove ineffectual, it then becomes his duty to call by name any member who obstinately persists in irregularity; whereupon the assembly may require such member to withdraw; who is then to be heard, if he desires it, in exculpation and to withdraw; then the presiding officer states the offence committed, and the assembly considers of the kind and degree of punishment to be inflicted.

226. If, on repeated trials, the presiding officer finds that the assembly will not support

him in the exercise of his authority, he will then be justified, but not till then, in permitting, without censure, every kind of disorder.

SECT. VI. AS TO DISORDERLY WORDS.

227. If a member, in speaking, makes use of language, which is personally offensive to another, or insulting to the assembly, and the member offended, or any other, thinks proper to complain of it to the assembly, the course of proceeding is as follows: [¶ 334.]

228. The member speaking is immediately interrupted in the course of his speech, by another or several members rising and calling to order; and, the member, who objects or complains of the words, is then called upon by the presiding officer to state the words which he complains of, repeating them exactly as he conceives them to have been spoken, in order that they may be reduced to writing by the clerk; or the member complaining, without being so called upon, may proceed at once to state the words either verbally or in writing, and desire that the clerk may take them down at the table. The presiding officer may then direct the clerk to take them

down; but if he sees the objection to be a trivial one, and thinks there is no foundation for their being thought disorderly, he will prudently delay giving any such directions, in order not unnecessarily to interrupt the proceedings; though if the members generally seem to be in favor of having the words taken down, by calling out to that effect, or by a vote, which the assembly may doubtless pass, the presiding officer should certainly order the clerk to take them down, in the form and manner in which they are stated by the member who objects.

229. The words objected to being thus written down, and forming a part of the minutes in the clerk's book, they are next to be read to the member who was speaking, who may deny that those are the words which he spoke, in which case, the assembly must decide by a question, whether they are the words or not[1]. If he does not deny that he spoke those words, or when the assembly has itself determined what the words are, then the member may either

---

[1] The words, as written down, may be amended, so as to conform to what the assembly thinks to be the truth.

justify them, or explain the sense in which he used them, so as to remove the objection of their being disorderly; or he may make an apology for them.

230. If the justification, or explanation, or apology, of the member, is thought sufficient by the assembly, no further proceeding is necessary; the member may resume and go on with his speech, the assembly being presumed, unless some further motion is made, to be satisfied; but, if any two members (one to make and the other to second the motion) think it necessary to state a question, so as to take the sense of the assembly upon the words, and whether the member in using them has been guilty of any offence towards the assembly, the member must withdraw before that question is stated; and then the sense of the assembly must be taken, and such further proceedings had in relation to punishing the member, as may be thought necessary and proper.

231. The above is the course of proceeding established by the writers of greatest authority[1], and ought invariably to be pursued; it

---

[1] Mr. Hatsell, in England, and Mr. Jefferson, in this country.

might however be improved, by the member who objects to words writing them down at once, and thereupon moving that they be made a part of the minutes; by which means, the presiding officer would be relieved from the responsibility of determining, in the first instance, upon the character of the words.

232. If offensive words are not taken notice of at the time they are spoken[1], but the member is allowed to finish his speech, and then any other person speaks, or any other matter of business intervenes, before notice is taken of the words which gave offence, the words are not to be written down, or the member using them censured. This rule is established for the common security of all the members; and to prevent the mistakes which must necessarily happen, if words complained of are not immediately reduced to writing.

---

1 Mr. Jefferson (§ 17) lays it down, that "disorderly words are not to be noticed till the member has finished his speech." But in this, he is contradicted by Hatsell, as well as by the general practice of legislative bodies.

CHAPTER XIII.

OF THE QUESTION.

233. When any proposition is made to a deliberative assembly, it is called a *motion;* when it is stated or propounded to the assembly, for their acceptance or rejection, it is denominated a *question;* and, when adopted, it becomes the *order*, *resolution*, or *vote*, of the assembly.

234. All the proceedings, which have thus far been considered, have only had for their object to bring a proposition into a form to be put to the question; that is, to be adopted as the sense, will, or judgment, of the assembly, or to be rejected; according as such proposition may be found to unite in its favor, or to fail of uniting, a majority of the members.

235. When any proposition, whether principal, subsidiary, or incidental, or of whatever nature it may be, is made, seconded, and stated, if no alteration is proposed, — or if it admits of none, or if it is amended, — and the debate upon it, if any, appears to be brought

to a close, the presiding officer then inquires, whether the assembly is ready for the question? and, if no person rises, the question is then stated, and the votes of the assembly taken upon it. [¶ 335.]

236. The question is not always stated to the assembly, in the precise form in which it arises or is introduced; thus, for example, when a member presents a petition, or the chairman of a committee offers a report, the question which arises, if no motion is made, is, *Shall the petition or the report be received?* and, so, when the previous question is moved, it is stated in this form, *Shall the main question be now put?* — the question being stated, in all cases, in the form in which it will appear on the journal, if it passes in the affirmative.

237. In matters of trifling importance, or which are generally of course, such as receiving petitions and reports, withdrawing motions, reading papers, &c., the presiding officer most commonly supposes or takes for granted the consent of the assembly, where no objection is expressed, and does not go through the formality of taking the question by a vote.* But if, after a vote has been taken in this informal way and declared, any

* [¶ 313.]

member rises to object, the presiding officer should consider every thing that has passed as nothing, and, at once, go back and pursue the regular course of proceeding. Thus, if a petition is received, without a question, and the clerk is proceeding to read it, in the usual order of business, if any one rises to object, it will be the safest and most proper course, for the presiding officer to require a motion for receiving it to be regularly made and seconded.

238. The question being stated by the presiding officer, he first puts it in the affirmative, namely: *As many as are of opinion that*— repeating the words of the question,—*say aye;* and, immediately, all the members who are of that opinion answer *aye;* the presiding officer then puts the question negatively; *As many as are of a different opinion, say no;* and, thereupon, all the members who are of that opinion answer *no.* The presiding officer judges by his ear which side has "the more voices," and decides accordingly, that *the ayes have it,* or *the noes have it,* as the case may be. If the presiding officer is doubtful as to the majority of voices, he may put the question a second time, and if he is still unable to decide, or, if, having decided according to his judg-

ment, any member rises and declares, that he believes the *ayes* or the *noes* (whichever it may be) *have it*, contrary to the declaration of the presiding officer[1], then the presiding officer directs the assembly to divide, in order that the members on the one side and the other may be counted.

239. If, however, any new motion should be made, after the presiding officer's declaration, or, if a member, who was not in the assembly-room when the question was taken, should come in, it will then be too late to contradict the presiding officer, and have the assembly divided.

240. The above is the parliamentary form of taking a question, and is in general use in this country; but, in some of our legislative assemblies, and especially in those of the New England states, the suffrages are given by the members holding up their right hands, first, those in the affirmative, and then those in the negative, of the question. If the presiding officer cannot determine, by the show of hands, which side has the majority, he may call upon the members to vote again, and if

---

1 The most common expression is: "I doubt the vote," or, "that vote is doubted."

he is still in doubt, or if his declaration is questioned, a division takes place. When the question is taken in this manner, the presiding officer directs the members, first on the affirmative side, and then on the negative, to manifest their opinion by holding up the right hand.

241. When a division of the assembly takes place, the presiding officer sometimes directs the members to range themselves on different sides of the assembly-room, and either counts them himself, or they are counted by tellers appointed by him for the purpose, or by monitors permanently appointed for that and other purposes; or the members rise in their seats, first on the affirmative and then on the negative, and (standing uncovered) are counted in the same manner. When the members are counted by the presiding officer, he announces the numbers and declares the result. When they are counted by tellers or monitors, the tellers must first agree among themselves, and then the one who has told for the majority reports the numbers to the presiding officer, who, thereupon, declares the result.

242. The best mode of dividing an assembly, that is at all numerous, is for the presiding

officer to appoint tellers for each division or section of the assembly-room, and then to require the members, first those in the affirmative, and then those in the negative, to rise, stand uncovered, and be counted; this being done, on each side, the tellers of the several divisions make their returns, and the presiding officer declares the result.

243. If the members are equally divided, the presiding officer may, if he pleases, give the casting vote;* or, if he chooses, he may refrain from voting, in which case, the motion does not prevail, and the decision is in the negative.

244. It is a general rule, that every member, who is in the assembly-room, at the time when the question is stated, has not only the right but is bound to vote; and, on the other hand, that no member can vote, who was not in the room at that time.

245. The only other form of taking the question, which requires to be described, is one in general use in this country, by means of which the names of the members voting on the one side and on the other are ascertained and entered in the journal of the assembly. This mode, which is peculiar to the legislative bodies of the United States, is called taking the

* [See ¶ 336, for Explanation of ¶ 243.]

question by yeas and nays. In order to take a question in this manner, it is stated on both sides at once, namely: *As many as are of opinion, that, &c., will, when their names are called, answer yes;* and, *As many as are of a different opinion will, when their names are called, answer no;* the roll of the assembly is then called over by the clerk, and each member, as his name is called, rises in his place, and answers *yes* or *no*, and the clerk notes the answer as the roll is called. When the roll has been gone through, the clerk reads over first the names of those who have answered in the affirmative, and then the names of those who have answered in the negative, in order that if he has made any mistake in noting the answer, or if any member has made a mistake in his answer, the mistake of either may be corrected. The names having been thus read over, and the mistakes, if any, corrected, the clerk counts the numbers on each side, and reports them to the presiding officer, who declares the result to the assembly.

246. The following is the mode practised in the house of representatives of Massachusetts, (which is by far the most numerous of all the legislative bodies in this country,) of taking a

question by yeas and nays. The names of the members being printed on a sheet, the clerk calls them in their order; and, as each one answers, the clerk (responding to the member, at the same time) places a figure in pencil, expressing the number of the answer, at the left or right of the name, according as the answer is yes or no; so that the last figure or number, on each side, shows the number of the answers on that side; and the two last numbers or figures represent the respective numbers of the affirmatives and negatives on the division. Thus, at the left hand of the name of the member who first answers *yes*, the clerk places a figure 1; at the right hand of the first member who answers *no*, he also places a figure 1; the second member that answers *yes* is marked 2; and so on to the end of the list; the side of the name, on which the figure is placed, denoting whether the answer is *yes* or *no*, and the figure denoting the number of the answer on that side. The affirmatives and negatives are then read separately, if necessary, though this is usually omitted, and the clerk is then prepared, by means of the last figure on each side, to give the numbers to the speaker to be announced to the house.

The names and answers are afterwards re corded on the journal.

247. In any of the modes of taking a ques tion, in which it is first put on one side, and then on the other, it is no full question, until the negative as well as the affirmative has been put. Consequently, until the negative has been put, it is in order for any member, in the same manner as if the division had not commenced, to rise and speak, make motions for amendment, or otherwise, and thus renew the debate; and, this, whether such member was in the assembly-room or not, when the question was put and partly taken. In such a case, the question must be put over again on the affirmative, as well as the negative side; for the reason, that members who were not in the assembly-room, when the question was first put, may have since come in, and also that some of those who voted, may have since changed their minds. When a question is taken by yeas and nays, and the negative as well as the affirmative of the question is stated, and the voting on each side begins and proceeds, at the same time, the question cannot be opened and the debate renewed, after the voting has commenced

248. If any question arises, in a point of order, as, for example, as to the right or the duty of a member to vote, during a division, the presiding officer must decide it peremptorily, subject to the revision and correction of the assembly, after the division is over. In a case of this kind, there can be no debate, though the presiding officer may if he pleases receive the assistance of members with their advice, which they are to give sitting, in order to avoid even the appearance of a debate; but this can only be with the leave of the presiding officer, as otherwise the division might be prolonged to an inconvenient length; nor can any question be taken, for otherwise there might be division upon division without end.

249. When, from counting the assembly on a division, it appears that there is not a quorum present, there is no decision; but the matter in question continues in the same state, in which it was before the division; and, when afterwards resumed, whether on the same or on some future day, it must be taken up at that precise point.

CHAPTER XIV.

OF RECONSIDERATION.

250. It is a principle of parliamentary law, upon which many of the rules and proceedings previously stated are founded, that when a question has been once put to a deliberative assembly, and decided, whether in the affirmative or negative, that decision is the judgment of the assembly, and cannot be again brought into question.

251. This principle holds equally, although the question proposed is not the identical question which has already been decided, but only its equivalent; as, for example, where the negative of one question amounts to the affirmative of the other, and leaves no other alternative, these questions are the equivalents of one another, and a decision of the one necessarily concludes the other.

252. A common application of the rule as to equivalent questions occurs in the case of an amendment proposed by striking out words: in which it is the invariable practice to

consider the negative of striking out as equivalent to the affirmative of agreeing; so that to put a question on agreeing, after a question on striking out is negatived, would be, in effect, to put the same question twice over.

253. The principle above stated does not apply so as to prevent putting the same question in the different stages of any proceeding, as, for example, in legislative bodies, the different stages of a bill; so, in considering reports of committees, questions already taken and decided, before the subject was referred, may be again proposed; and, in like manner, orders of the assembly, and instructions or references to committees, may be discharged or rescinded.

254. The inconvenience of this rule, which is still maintained in all its strictness in the British parliament (though divers expedients are there resorted to, to counteract or evade it), has led to the introduction into the parliamentary practice of this country of the motion for *reconsideration;* which, while it recognizes and upholds the rule in all its ancient strictness, yet allows a deliberative assembly, for sufficient reasons, to relieve itself from the embarrassment and inconvenience, which

would occasionally result from a strict enforcement of the rule in a particular case.

255. It has now come to be a common practice in all our deliberative assemblies, and may consequently be considered as a principle of the common parliamentary law of this country, to reconsider a vote already passed, whether affirmatively or negatively.

256. For this purpose, a motion is made and seconded, in the usual manner, that such a vote be reconsidered; and, if this motion prevails, the matter stands before the assembly in precisely the same state and condition, and the same questions are to be put in relation to it, as if the vote reconsidered had never been passed. Thus, if an amendment by inserting words is moved and rejected, the same amendment cannot be moved again; but, the assembly may reconsider the vote by which it was rejected, and then the question will recur on the amendment, precisely as if the former vote had never been passed.

257. It is usual in legislative bodies, to regulate by a special rule the time, manner, and by whom, a motion to reconsider may be made; thus, for example, that it shall be made only on the same or a succeeding day, — by a

member who voted with the majority, — or at a time when there are as many members present as there were when the vote was passed; but, where there is no special rule on the subject, a motion to reconsider must be considered in the same light as any other motion, and as subject to no other rules. [¶ 337.]

CHAPTER XV.

OF COMMITTEES.

SECT. I. THEIR NATURE AND FUNCTIONS.

258. It is usual in all deliberative assemblies, to take the preliminary (sometimes, also, the intermediate) measures, and to prepare matters to be acted upon, in the assembly, by means of committees, composed either of members specially selected for the particular occasion, or appointed beforehand for all matters of the same nature.

259. Committees of the first kind are usually called *select*, the others *standing;* though the former appellation belongs with equal propriety to both, in order to distinguish them from another form of committee, constituted either for a particular occasion, or for all cases of a certain kind, which is composed of all the members of the assembly, and therefore denominated a *committee of the whole*

260. The advantages of proceeding in this mode are manifold. It enables a deliberative assembly to do many things, which, from its

numbers, it would otherwise be unable to do; to accomplish a much greater quantity of business, by dividing it among the members, than could possibly be accomplished, if the whole body were obliged to devote itself to each particular subject; — and to act in the preliminary and preparatory steps, with a greater degree of freedom, than is compatible with the forms of proceeding usually observed in full assembly.

261. Committees are appointed to consider a particular subject, either at large or under special instructions; to obtain information in reference to a matter before the assembly, either by personal inquiry and inspection, or by the examination of witnesses; and to digest and put into the proper form, for the adoption of the assembly, all resolutions, votes, orders, and other papers, with which they may be charged. Committees are commonly said to be the "eyes and ears" of the assembly; it is equally true, that, for certain purposes, they are also its "head and hands."

262. The powers and functions of committees depend chiefly upon the general authority and particular instructions given them by the assembly, at the time of their appointment;

but they may also be, and very often are, further instructed, whilst they are in the exercise of their functions; and, sometimes, it even happens, that these additional instructions wholly change the nature of a committee, by charging it with inquiries quite different from those for which it was originally established.

SECT. II. THEIR APPOINTMENT.

263. In the manner of appointing committees, there is no difference between standing and other select committees, as to the mode of selecting the members to compose them; and, in reference to committees of the whole, as there is no selection of members, they are appointed simply by the order of the assembly.

264. In the appointment of select committees, the first thing to be done is to fix upon the number. This is usually effected in the same manner that blanks are filled, namely, by members proposing, without the formality of a motion, such numbers as they please, which are then separately put to the question, beginning with the largest and going regularly through to the smallest, until the assembly comes to a vote.

265. The number being settled, there are :hree modes of selecting the members, to wit,)y the appointment of the presiding officer, —)y ballot, — and by nomination and vote of :he assembly; the first, sometimes in virtue)f a standing rule, sometimes in pursuance of ı vote of the assembly in a particular case; he second always in pursuance of a vote; he last is the usual course where no vote s taken.

266. In deliberative assemblies, whose sittings are of considerable length, as legislative odies, it is usual to provide by a standing ule, that, unless otherwise ordered in a paricular case, all committees shall be named y the presiding officer. Where this is the :ase, whenever a committee is ordered, and he number settled, the presiding officer at nce names the members to compose it. Sometimes, also, the rule fixes the number, f which, unless otherwise ordered, committees shall consist. This mode of appointing . committee is frequently resorted to, where here is no rule on the subject.

267. When a committee is ordered to be :ppointed by ballot, the members are chosen y the assembly, either singly or all together,

as may be ordered, in the same manner that other elections are made; and, in such elections, as in other cases of the election of the officers of the assembly, a majority of all the votes given in is necessary to a choice.

268. When a committee is directed to be appointed by nomination and vote, the names of the members proposed are put to the question singly, and approved or rejected by the assembly, by a vote taken in the usual manner. If the nomination is directed to be made by the presiding officer, he may propose the names in the same manner, or all at once; the former mode being the most direct and simple; the latter enabling the assembly to vote more understandingly upon the several names proposed. When the nomination is directed to be made at large, the presiding officer calls upon the assembly to nominate, and names being mentioned accordingly, he puts to vote the first name he hears.

269. It is also a compendious mode of appointing a committee, to revive one which has already discharged itself by a report; or by charging a committee appointed for one purpose with some additional duty, of the same or a different character.

270. In regard to the appointment of committees, so far as the selection of the members is concerned, it is a general rule in legislative bodies, when a bill is to be referred, that none who speak directly against the body of it are to be of the committee, for the reason, that he who would totally destroy will not amend; but, that, for the opposite reason, those who only take exceptions to some particulars in the bill are to be of the committee. This rule supposes the purpose of the commitment to be, not the consideration of the general merits of the bill, but the amendment of it in its particular provisions, so as to make it acceptable to the assembly.

271. This rule, of course, is only for the guidance of the presiding officer, and the members, in the exercise of their discretion; as the assembly may refuse to excuse from serving, or may itself appoint, on a committee, persons who are opposed to the subject referred. It is customary, however, in all deliberative assemblies, to constitute a committee of such persons, (the mover and seconder of a measure being of course appointed,) a majority of whom, at least, are favorably inclined to the measure proposed.

272. When a committee has been appointed, in reference to a particular subject, it is the duty of the secretary of the assembly to make out a list of the members, together with a certified copy of the authority or instructions under which they are to act, and to give the papers to the member first named on the list of the committee, if convenient, but, otherwise, to any other member of the committee.

Sect. III. Their Organization and Manner of proceeding.

273. The person first named on a committee acts as its chairman, or presiding officer, so far as relates to the preliminary steps to be taken, and is usually permitted to do so, through the whole proceedings; but this is a matter of courtesy; every committee having a right to elect its own chairman, who presides over it, and makes the report of its proceedings to the assembly.

274. A committee is properly to receive directions from the assembly, as to the time and place of its meeting, and cannot regularly sit at any other time or place; and it may be ordered to sit immediately, whilst the assembly is sitting, and make its report forthwith.

275. When no directions are given, a committee may select its own time and place of meeting; but, without a special order to that effect, it is not at liberty to sit whilst the assembly sits; and, if a committee is sitting, when the assembly comes to order after an adjournment, it is the duty of the chairman to rise, instantly, on being certified of it, and, with the other members, to attend the service of the assembly.

276. In regard to its forms of proceeding, a committee is essentially a miniature assembly; — it can only act when regularly assembled together, as a committee, and not by separate consultation and consent of the members; nothing being the agreement or report of a committee, but what is agreed to in that manner; — a vote taken in committee is as binding as a vote of the assembly; — a majority of the members is necessary to constitute a quorum for business, unless a larger or smaller number has been fixed by the assembly itself, — and a committee has full power over whatever may be committed to it, except that it is not at liberty to change the title or subject.*

277. A committee, which is under no directions as to the time and place of meeting, may

10

* [¶ 338.]

meet when and where it pleases, and adjourn itself from day to day, or otherwise, until it has gone through with the business committed to it; but, if it is ordered to meet at a particular time, and it fails of doing so, for any cause, the committee is closed, and cannot act without being newly directed to sit.

278. Disorderly words spoken in a committee must be written down in the same manner as in the assembly; but the committee, as such, can do nothing more than report them to the assembly for its animadversion; neither can a committee punish disorderly conduct of any other kind, but must report it to the assembly

279. When any paper is before a committee whether select or of the whole, it may either have originated with the committee, or have been referred to them; and, in either case, when the paper comes to be considered, the course is for it to be first read entirely through, by the clerk of the committee, if there is one, otherwise by the chairman; and then to be read through again by paragraphs, by the chairman, pausing at the end of each paragraph, and putting questions for amending, either by striking out or inserting, if proposed. This is

the natural order of proceeding in considering and amending any paper, and is to be strictly adhered to in the assembly; but the same strictness does not seem necessary in a committee.

280. If the paper before a committee is one which has originated with the committee, questions are put on amendments proposed, but not on agreeing to the several paragraphs of which it is composed, separately, as they are gone through with; this being reserved for the close, when a question is to be put on the whole, for agreeing to the paper, as amended, or unamended.

281. If the paper be one, which has been referred to the committee, they proceed as in the other case to put questions of amendment, if proposed, but no final question on the whole; because all parts of the paper, having been passed upon if not adopted by the assembly as the basis of its action, stand, of course, unless altered or struck out by a vote of the assembly. And even if the committee are opposed to the whole paper, and are of opinion, that it cannot be made good by amendments, they have no authority to reject it; they must report it back to the assembly,

without amendments, (specially stating their objections, if they think proper,) and there make their opposition as individual members[1].

282. In the case of a paper originating with a committee, they may erase or interline it as much as they please; though, when finally agreed to, it ought to be reported in a clear draft, fairly written, without erasure or interlineation.

283. But, in the case of a paper referred to a committee, they are not at liberty to erase, interline, blot, disfigure, or tear it, in any manner; but they must, in a separate paper, set down the amendments they have agreed to report, stating the words which are to be inserted or omitted, and the places where the amendments are to be made, by references to the paragraph or section, line, and word.

284. If the amendments agreed to are very numerous and minute, the committee may report them altogether, in the form of a new and amended draft.

285. When a committee has gone through the paper, or agreed upon a report on the

---

[1] This rule is not applicable, of course, to those cases in which the *subject*, as well as the *form or details* of a paper, is referred to the committee.

subject, which has been referred to them, it is then moved by some member, and thereupon voted, that the committee rise, and that the chairman, or some other member, make their report to the assembly.

SECT. IV. THEIR REPORT.

286. When the report of a committee is to be made, the chairman, or member appointed to make the report, standing in his place, informs the assembly, that the committee, to whom was referred such a subject or paper, have, according to order, had the same under consideration, and have directed him to make a report thereon, or to report the same with sundry amendments, or without amendment, as the case may be, which he is ready to do, when the assembly shall please; and he or any other member may then move that the report be now received. On this motion being made, the question is put whether the assembly will receive the report at that time: and a vote passes, accordingly, either to receive it then, or fixing upon some future time for its reception. [¶ 339.]

287. At the time, when, by the order of the assembly, the report is to be received, the chairman reads it in his place, and then delivers it, together with all the papers, connected with it, to the clerk at the table; where it is again read, and then lies on the table, until the time assigned, or until it suits the convenience of the assembly, to take it up for consideration.

288. If the report of the committee is of a paper with amendments, the chairman reads the amendments with the coherence in the paper, whatever it may be, and opens the alterations, and the reasons of the committee for the amendments, until he has gone through the whole; and, when the report is read at the clerk's table, the amendments only are read without the coherence.

239. In practice, however, the formality of a motion and vote on the reception of a report is usually dispensed with; though, if any objection is made, or if the presiding officer sees any informality in the report, he should decline receiving it without a motion and vote; and a report, if of any considerable length, is seldom read, either by the chairman in his place, or by the clerk at the table, until

it is taken up for consideration. In legislative assemblies, the printing of reports generally renders the reading of them unnecessary.

290. The report of a committee being made and received, the committee is dissolved, and can act no more without a new power; but their authority may be revived by a vote, and the same matter recommitted to them. If a report, when offered to the assembly, is not received, the committee is not thereby discharged, but may be ordered to sit again, and a time and place appointed accordingly.

291. When a subject or paper has been once committed, and a report made upon it, it may be recommitted either to the same or a different committee; and if a report is recommitted, before it has been agreed to by the assembly, what has heretofore passed in the committee is of no validity; the whole question being again before the committee, as if nothing had passed there in relation to it.

292. The report of a committee may be made in three different forms, namely: *first*, it may contain merely a statement of facts, reasoning, or opinion, in relation to the subject of it, without any specific conclusion; or, *second*, a statement of facts, reasoning, or

opinion, concluding with a resolution, or series of resolutions, or some other specific proposition; or, *third*, it may consist merely of such resolutions, or propositions, without any introductory part.

293. The first question, on a report, is, in strictness, on receiving it; though, in practice, this question is seldom or never made; the consent of the assembly, especially in respect to the report of a committee of the whole, being generally presumed, unless objection is made. When a report is received, whether by general consent, or upon a question and vote, the committee is discharged, and the report becomes the basis of the future proceedings of the assembly, on the subject to which it relates.

294. At the time assigned for the consideration of a report, it may be treated and disposed of precisely like any other proposition (59 to 77); and may be amended, in the same manner (78 to 133), both in the preliminary statement, reasoning, or opinion, if it contain any, and in the resolutions, or other propositions with which it concludes; so if it consist merely of a statement, &c., without resolutions, or of resolutions, &c., without any introductory part.

295. The final question on a report, whatever form it may have, is usually stated on its acceptance; and, when accepted, the whole report is adopted by the assembly, and becomes the statement, reasoning, opinion, resolution, or other act, as the case may be, of the assembly; the doings of a committee, when agreed to, adopted, or accepted, becoming the acts of the assembly, in the same manner as if done originally by the assembly itself, without the intervention of a committee.

296. It would be better, however, and in stricter accordance with parliamentary rules, to state the final question on a report, according to the form of it. If the report contain merely a statement of facts, reasoning, or opinion, the question should be on acceptance; if it also conclude with resolutions, or other specific propositions, of any kind, — the introductory part being consequently merged in the conclusion, — the question should be on agreeing to the resolutions, or on adopting the order, or other proposition, or on passing or coming to the vote, recommended by the committee; and the same should be the form of the question, when the report consists merely of resolutions, &c., without any introductory part.

SECT. V. COMMITTEE OF THE WHOLE.

297. When a subject has been ordered to be referred to a committee of the whole, the form of going from the assembly into committee, is, for the presiding officer, at the time appointed for the committee to sit, on motion made and seconded for the purpose, to put the question that the assembly do now resolve itself into a committee of the whole, to take under consideration such a matter, naming it. If this question is determined in the affirmative, the result is declared by the presiding officer, who, naming some member to act as chairman of the committee, then leaves the chair, and takes a seat elsewhere, like any other member; and the person appointed chairman seats himself (not in the chair of the assembly but) at the clerk's table.

298. The chairman named by the presiding officer is generally acquiesced in by the committee; though, like all other committees, a committee of the whole have a right to elect a chairman for themselves, some member, by general consent, putting the question. [¶ 340.]

299. The same number of members is necessary to constitute a quorum of a committee of the whole, as of the assembly; and if the members present fall below a quorum, at any time, in the course of the proceedings, the chairman, on a motion and question, rises, — the presiding officer thereupon resumes the chair, — and the chairman informs the assembly (he can make no other report) of the cause of the dissolution of the committee.

300. When the assembly is in committee of the whole, it is the duty of the presiding officer to remain in the assembly-room, in order to be at hand to resume the chair, in case the committee should be broken up by some disorder, or for want of a quorum, or should rise, either to report progress, or to make their final report upon the matter committed to them

301. The clerk of the assembly does not act as clerk of the committee (this is the duty of the assistant clerk in legislative bodies), or record in his journal any of the proceedings or votes of the committee, but only their report as made to the assembly.

302. The proceedings in a committee of the whole, though, in general, similar to those

in the assembly itself, and in other committees, are yet different in some respects, the principal of which are the following: —

303. *First.* The previous question cannot be moved in a committee of the whole. The only means of avoiding an improper discussion is, to move that the committee rise; and, if it is apprehended, that the same discussion will be attempted on returning again into committee, the assembly can discharge the committee, and proceed itself with the business, keeping down any improper discussion by means of the previous question[1].

304. *Second.* A committee of the whole cannot adjourn, like other committees, to some other time or place, for the purpose of going on with and completing the consideration of the subject referred to them; but, if their business is unfinished, at the usual time for the assembly to adjourn, or, for any other reason, they wish to proceed no further at a particular time, the form of proceeding is, for some member to move that the committee rise, — report progress, — and ask leave to sit

[1] If the object be to stop debate, that can only be effected, in the same manner, unless there is a special rule, as to the time of speaking, or to taking a subject out of committee.

again; and, if this motion prevails, the chairman rises, — the presiding officer resumes the chair of the assembly, — and the chairman of the committee informs him that the committee of the whole have, according to order, had under their consideration such a matter, and have made some progress therein[1]; but, not having had time to go through with the same, have directed him to ask leave for the committee to sit again. The presiding officer thereupon puts a question on giving the committee leave to sit again, and also on the time when the assembly will again resolve itself into a committee. If leave to sit again is not granted, the committee is of course dissolved.

305. *Third.* In a committee of the whole, every member may speak as often as he pleases, provided he can obtain the floor; whereas, in the assembly itself, no member can speak more than once.

306. *Fourth.* A committee of the whole cannot refer any matter to another committee; but other committees may and do frequently exercise their functions, and expedite their

---

[1] If it is a second time, the expression is, "some further progress," &c.

business, by means of sub-committees of their own members.

307. *Fifth.* In a committee of the whole, the presiding officer of the assembly has a right to take a part in the debate and proceedings, in the same manner as any other member.

308. *Sixth.* A committee of the whole, like a select committee, has no authority to punish a breach of order, whether of a member, or stranger; but can only rise and report the matter to the assembly, who may proceed to punish the offender. Disorderly words must be written down in committee, in the same manner as in the assembly, and reported to the assembly for their animadversion.

309. The foregoing are the principal points of difference between proceedings in the assembly and in committees of the whole; in most other respects they are precisely similar. It is sometimes said, that in a committee of the whole, it is not necessary that a motion should be seconded. There is no foundation, however, either in reason or parliamentary usage, for this opinion.

310. When a committee of the whole have gone through with the matter referred to them,

a member moves that the committee rise, and that the chairman (or some other member) report their proceedings to the assembly; which being resolved, the chairman rises and goes to his place, — the presiding officer resumes the chair of the assembly, — and the chairman informs him, that the committee have gone through with the business referred to them, and that he is ready to make their report, when the assembly shall think proper to receive it. The time for receiving the report is then agreed upon; and, at the time appointed, it is made and received in the same manner as that of any other committee (286).

311. It sometimes happens, that the formality of a motion and question as to the time of receiving a report is dispensed with. If the assembly are ready to receive it, at the time, they cry out, "now, now," whereupon the chairman proceeds; if not then ready, some other time is mentioned, as "to-morrow," or "Monday," and that time is fixed by general consent. But, when it is not the general sense of the assembly to receive the report at the time, it is better to agree upon and fix the time by a motion and question.

CONCLUDING REMARKS.

312. In bringing this treatise to a close, it will not be deemed out of place, to make a suggestion or two for the benefit of those persons, who may be called upon to act as presiding officers, for the first time.

313. One of the most essential parts of the duty of a presiding officer is, to give the closest attention to the proceedings of the assembly, and, especially, to what is said by every member who speaks. Without the first, confusion will be almost certain to occur; wasting the time, perhaps disturbing the harmony, of the assembly. The latter is not merely a decent manifestation of respect for those who have elevated him to an honorable station; but it tends greatly to encourage timid or diffident members, and to secure them a

patient and attentive hearing; and it often enables the presiding officer, by a timely interference, to check offensive language, in season to prevent scenes of tumult and disorder, such as have sometimes disgraced our legislative halls.

314 It should be constantly kept in mind by a presiding officer, that, in a deliberative assembly, there can regularly be but one thing done or doing, at the same time. This caution he will find particularly useful to him, whenever a quarrel arises between two members, in consequence of words spoken in debate. In such a case, he will do well to require that the regular course of proceeding shall be strictly pursued; and will take care to restrain members from interfering in any other manner. In general, the solemnity and deliberation, with which this mode is attended, will do much to allay heat and excitement, and to restore harmony and order to the assembly.

315. A presiding officer will often find himself embarrassed, by the difficulty, as well as the delicacy, of deciding points of order, or giving directions as to the manner of

proceeding. In such cases, it will be useful for him to recollect, that—

THE GREAT PURPOSE OF ALL RULES AND FORMS, IS TO SUBSERVE THE WILL OF THE ASSEMBLY RATHER THAN TO RESTRAIN IT; TO FACILITATE, AND NOT TO OBSTRUCT, THE EXPRESSION OF THEIR DELIBERATE SENSE.

ADDITIONS AND CORRECTIONS.

§ 21. General Consent.

[The sign §, at the head of a note, refers to the paragraph in the body of the work to which the note belongs.]

316. The terms, "general consent," as used in parliamentary practice, denote the unanimous opinion of the assembly, when their opinion is expressed informally, and not by means of a vote. Whenever, therefore, it is said, that the general consent of the assembly is necessary to the adoption of any measure, it is to be understood, that if the question is proposed informally, no objection must be made to it, or that if proposed in a formal manner, the vote in its favor must be unanimous.

§ 51. Reading Petition.

317. When a petition has been received, the next step in the proceedings is the reading of it by the clerk, for the information of the assembly; which, though in the usual course of business, and not likely to be objected to, after the petition has been received, is nevertheless the subject of a motion and question, to be regularly submitted to

the assembly and voted upon; and, until a petition has been read, no order can properly be made respecting it, not even for its lying on the table.

§ 55. Secondary Motion.

318. An exception to the general rule, requiring motions to be seconded, occurs, when it is proposed to proceed with, or to execute, or to enforce, an order of the assembly; as, for example, when it is moved to proceed with an order of the day, or when a member suggests or calls for the enforcement of some order relating to the observance of decorum, or the regularity of proceeding. Thus, in the English house of commons, a single member may require the enforcement of the standing order for the exclusion of strangers; and, so, when the second or other reading of a bill is made the order for a particular day, a motion, on that day, to read the bill according to the order, need not be seconded.

§ 56. Before Statement of Motion from the Chair.

319. The principle stated in this paragraph, must not be understood to preclude all proceeding with, or allusion to, a motion, until it has been stated from the chair. On the contrary, after a motion has been made, or made and seconded, but not yet proposed as a question, it is competent for the mover to withdraw or modify it, either of himself, or on the suggestion of some

other member, or of the presiding officer, and without any motion or vote for the purpose. The rule only requires, that, until a motion is regularly seconded and stated, it should not be spoken to as a question for the decision of the assembly, or be made the subject of any motion or proceeding as such. While, therefore, the presiding officer should permit members to make remarks or suggestions, for the purposes alluded to, with reference to motions not yet stated, he should be careful to check and prevent all observations which may tend to excite debate; it being a general rule, that no debate can be allowed to take place on any subject, unless there is a question pending at the time.

§ 71. Lie on the Table.

320. When any motion or proposition, report, resolution, or other matter, has been ordered to lie on the table, it is not in strictness allowable to make any further order, with reference to the same subject, on the same day. The order may, however, be limited to a specific time; as, for example, until some other topic or subject is disposed of.

The proper motion, for proceeding with a matter which has been ordered to lie on the table, is, that the assembly do now proceed to consider that matter or subject. The motion sometimes made, is, that the subject be taken up, or taken up for consideration.

§ 75. Authority of Committee.

321. The authority of a committee, in reference to the subject matter referred to its consideration, as well as to the time and manner of its proceeding, depends wholly upon, and is derived from, the order by which the committee is instituted. It can only consider the matter referred to it; and, consequently, is not at liberty, like the assembly itself, to change the subject under consideration by means of an amendment. This rule is equally applicable to committees of the whole.

§ 92, 93. Modification or Amendment of a Motion by the Mover.

322. Before a motion has been stated, the mover, as already remarked (note to § 56), may modify or withdraw it at his pleasure; after it has been stated, he can only withdraw or modify it by general consent; he may, however, like any other member, move to amend. The acceptance by the mover, of an amendment moved or suggested by some other member, stands upon the same ground.

§ 112, 122. Amendments by Striking Out.

323. When the parliamentary form of putting the question, on a motion to strike or leave out words, is adopted, the question is first stated, that the words proposed to be struck out stand as part

of the motion. If this question passes in the negative, a question is then to be stated on inserting the words proposed, which may be amended like any other motion to insert or add words. If the question on the standing of the words passes in the affirmative, the residue of the motion to strike out and insert falls without a question. According to the parliamentary form, therefore, a motion to strike out and insert is necessarily divided. The remark of Mr. Jefferson, quoted in the note to § 122, that "the question, if desired, is then to be divided," &c., may be explained by supposing, that when a motion was made to strike out and insert, which was not objected to, the question was proposed in the terms of the motion; but, that, if objected to, it was then to be put, of course, in the parliamentary form. In the house of delegates of Virginia, of which Mr. Jefferson had been a member, the parliamentary form of stating the question was in use.

§ 128 to 133. Amendment changing the Nature of a Question.

324. In some legislative assemblies, the house of representatives of Massachusetts, for example, it is provided by a special rule, that no motion or proposition, relative to a different subject from the one under consideration, shall be admitted under color of an amendment. When a rule of this nature is in force, the assembly, by proceeding to consider a given subject, places itself

in the situation of a committee, to whom that subject is referred.

§ 137. Motion to Adjourn.

325. The reason, why a motion to adjourn, moved for the purpose of superseding or suppressing a pending question, is not susceptible of amendment, is, that if amended, it would at once become inadmissible, in point of order, on the ground of its being introductory to a second question, having no privilege to take the place of a question already pending and entitled to be first disposed of.

§ 143. Order of the Day.

See note to § 55.

§ 154. Questions of Order.

326. In the British parliament, the presiding officers do not appear to consider it their duty to decide points of order, unless appealed to by the house for that purpose; which, in the commons, is usually effected by a general cry of *chair* from the members; and, it is extremely rare, that an opinion, given in answer to such a call, is not submitted to by the house. If not satisfactory, the point of order may be separated from the main question, by a motion and question for the purpose, on which the presiding officer's decision may be overruled; or, without any distinct question being made, the house may proceed to pass

upon the point of order, as involved in the main question, and, in deciding the latter, may go contrary to the opinion of the presiding officer, upon the matter of order. In the legislative assemblies of this country, it is generally, if not universally, provided by a special rule, that every question of order shall, in the first instance, be decided by the presiding officer, subject to an appeal to the assembly itself. Such, also, appears to be the usage of deliberative assemblies, not legislative in their character. And, it is on these grounds of rule and usage, that the doctrine laid down in this paragraph is founded.

The statement, that questions of order are to be decided, in the first instance, by the presiding officer, without any previous debate or discussion by the assembly, must not be understood to mean, that the presiding officer is precluded from allowing members to express their opinions upon the point of order, before himself deciding it; but, merely, that the matter is not then to be debated and discussed, as a question to be decided by the assembly. The presiding officer, before expressing his own opinion, may, if he pleases, take the opinions of other members. It is manifest, however, that when he is ready to give his own opinion, he may proceed at once, and cannot be precluded from doing so by any other member claiming a right to be first heard.

§ 161. Withdrawal of a Motion.

327. A motion, when made, seconded, and stated, cannot be withdrawn without the general

consent, or, if put formally to the question, the unanimous vote of the assembly.

§ 198. See note to § 36.

§ 200. Interruption of a Member Speaking, by a Call to Order.

328. The rule stated in this paragraph, that a member speaking cannot rightfully be interrupted in his speech, but by a call to order, does not make it the duty of the presiding officer to refuse to hear a member, who rises and addresses the chair whilst another is speaking; for, if this were the case, the presiding officer could very rarely know whether there might not be occasion for the interruption; and would thus be in danger of keeping the assembly in ignorance of matters, which it might be of the highest concern for them to know. When, therefore, a member rises whilst another is speaking, and addresses the chair, he should inform the presiding officer that he rises to a point of order, or to the orders of the assembly, or to a matter of privilege. It will then be the duty of the presiding officer to direct the member speaking to suspend his remarks, or to resume his seat, and the member rising to proceed with the statement of his point or other matter of order, or of privilege. If the latter, on proceeding, discloses matter which shows that the interruption was proper, the subject so introduced must first be disposed of; and then the member who was interrupted, is to be directed to proceed

with his speech. If it appears that there was no sufficient ground for the interruption, the member rising is to be directed to resume his seat, and the member interrupted to proceed with his speech. Every member, therefore, possessing the right to interrupt another in his speech, on a proper occasion, any wanton abuse of this right, for the purpose of personal annoyance, is liable to censure and punishment; it being itself a breach of order unnecessarily and wantonly to call or interrupt another member to order.

In reference to the occasions, on which the interruption of a member speaking is allowed, it is to be observed, that they are not restricted, as the language of § 200 might seem to imply, to breaches of order in debate, on the part of the member speaking. Any matter of privilege, affecting the assembly itself, or any of its members, of which the assembly ought to have instant information, furnishes such an occasion; as, for example, where access to the place of sitting of the assembly is obstructed, or the person of a member is attacked; or where something connected with the proceeding of the assembly requires instant attention, as where it becomes necessary to have lights; or where something occurs relative to the member himself who is speaking, as where he is annoyed and disturbed by noise and disorder, or where, in consequence of his strength failing him, it becomes necessary that he should finish his speech sitting.

§ 207. Precedence in Speaking of the Presiding Officer.

329. The rule stated in this paragraph does not, of course, preclude the presiding officer from interrupting a member whilst speaking, whenever a proper occasion occurs for such an interruption; as, for example, when the member himself is guilty of a breach of order.

§ 209. Questions not Debatable.

330. In the legislative assemblies of this country, it is usual to provide by a special rule, that certain questions shall be decided without debate. Among these, the most common is the motion to adjourn. In the absence, however, of a special rule, restricting the right of debate in reference to some particular subject, every question, with the exception perhaps of those which require unanimity, that may be moved, may be debated. In both houses of parliament, important debates have frequently taken place on motions, as, for example, to adjourn, which, in the legislative assemblies of this country, would not generally be considered debatable.

§ 213. Several Questions involved in the Same Debate.

331. It sometimes happens, that a question under debate becomes enlarged rather than narrowed, by the introduction of a subsidiary motion; as, for example, when an amendment is moved, which involves in itself the merits of the original

proposition, in which case, the debate may embrace both.

§ 216. Speaking but Once to the Same Question.

332. The rule, stated in this and the preceding paragraphs, refers solely to the question technically considered, and is wholly irrespective of the subject matter. No member can speak more than once to the same question; but he may speak to the same subject, as often as it is presented in the form of a different question.

§ 218.

333. The expression in this paragraph, "to clear a matter of fact," denotes merely a statement, by a member who has already spoken, of facts which he considers it important for the assembly to be possessed of, before coming to a vote upon the question pending.

§ 227. Disorderly Words.

334. The offence of disorderly words may be committed, not only by language used in the course of debate, but also by words used in making a motion, or report.

§ 235. Statement of Motion.

335. Strictly speaking, no question can arise in a deliberative assembly, without a motion being first made and seconded; though, sometimes, for the dispatch of business, the presiding officer

takes it for granted that a proper and usual motion is made (when in fact it is not), and proposes a question accordingly.

§ 243. Right and Duty of Presiding Officer as to Voting.

336. The principle asserted in this paragraph, was laid down on the authority of the French translation of a little work of the late Sir Samuel Romilly (never published in English), on parliamentary practice, in which it is stated, that the speaker of the house of commons has his election to vote or not, when the house is equally divided. It appears quite certain, however, from an examination of the published debates and proceedings of the house of commons, that the speaker has no such election; and, consequently, either that the author was himself mistaken, or, which is more probable, that the translator mistook his author. Taking the practice of the house of commons as the best evidence of the general parliamentary law, — and this seems to be indisputable, — the rule laid down in § 243 should be modified accordingly, and thus stated, namely:

"If the members are equally divided, it then becomes the duty of the presiding officer to give the casting vote; in doing which, he may, if he pleases, give his reasons."

§ 250 to 257. Reconsideration.

337. Proceedings, analagous in principle to the motion for reconsideration, appear occasionally,

though very rarely, to have been admitted in the British parliament; but, it is believed, the motion to reconsider, as in use in this country, is of American origin. The motion is, in form, that such a vote be reconsidered; in substance, that the subject of that vote be again considered, upon the original motion, as if that motion had never been considered and passed upon. On the motion to reconsider, the whole subject is as much open for debate as if it had not been discussed at all; and, if the motion prevail, the subject is again open for debate on the original motion, in the same manner as if that motion had never been put to the question.

§ 276. Quorum of Committee.

338. The statement, contained in this paragraph, that a majority of the members of a committee is sufficient to constitute a quorum for proceeding with business, unless the number should be otherwise fixed by the assembly itself, was made upon the supposition, that, in this country, the rule had been so settled by usage. It should also have been stated, at the same time, as the parliamentary rule, that the presence of every member is essential, and that of a majority is not sufficient, to constitute a committee. In all places, therefore, where there is any doubt as to the existence of the usage, it will be proper that the number of the quorum should be fixed by the assembly itself, either by a general rule, or by the order for the appointment of the committee.

SECT. 286. REPORT OF COMMITTEE.

339. In this and the succeeding paragraphs, relating to the report of a committee, no notice is taken of what is commonly known in this country as a *minority report;* in reference to which, it being now a proceeding of frequent occurrence, though not strictly parliamentary, some explanation seems necessary and proper.

The report of a committee being the conclusion which is agreed to by a majority of the members, the dissenting or not-agreeing members, according to strict parliamentary practice, would have no other mode of bringing their views before the assembly, than as individual members. Inasmuch, however, as such members may be supposed to have given the subject equal consideration with the other members of the committee, and may, therefore, be in possession of views and opinions equally worthy of the attention of the assembly, the practice has become general in the legislative assemblies of this country, to allow members in the minority to present their views and conclusions in the parliamentary form of a report, which is accordingly known by the somewhat incongruous appellation of a minority report. Any two or more of the members may unite in such a report, or each one of them may express his views in a separate document.

A minority report is not recognized as a report of the committee, or acted upon as such; it is received by courtesy, and allowed to accompany the report, as representing the opinions of the minority; and, in order to its being adopted by the assembly, it must be moved as an amendment to the report, when that comes to be considered.

SECT. 297. CHAIRMAN OF COMMITTEE OF THE WHOLE.

340. The naming of the chairman of a committee of the whole, by the presiding officer, which is supposed to be the usual practice in the legislative assemblies of this country, ordinarily takes place in virtue of a special rule. Where this is the case, the member so named becomes the chairman of the committee. But, where there is no such rule, some member is called upon by one or more of the members of the committee to take the chair; and, if no objection is made, or no other member called to the chair, the member so designated becomes the chairman. If objection is made, or any other member is called to the chair, the chairman must be regularly chosen. But, in order to do this, the presiding officer should resume the chair, and the choice be made by the assembly, acting as such, and not in committee. The statement in § 298, that, where a chairman is to be appointed by vote, the question is to be put by some member in the committtee, though laid down by Mr. Jefferson, on the authority of an old writer on parliamentary proceedings, is not sanctioned by Hatsell, or borne out by the modern practice in the British parliament, in both houses of which the practice as above stated prevails.

INDEX.

**** The figures refer to the numbers of the paragraphs.*

www.ingramcontent.com/pod-product-compliance
Lightning Source LLC
LaVergne TN
LVHW011222110826
845150LV00006B/1511

* 9 7 8 1 4 2 5 5 1 5 4 8 5 *